CONFRONTING GLOBAL WARMING

Nature and Wildlife

CONFRONTING GLOBAL WARMING

Nature and Wildlife

Diane Andrews Henningfeld

Michael E. Mann
Consulting Editor

GREENHAVEN PRESS
A part of Gale, Cengage Learning

GALE
CENGAGE Learning™

Detroit • New York • San Francisco • New Haven, Conn • Waterville, Maine • London

GALE
CENGAGE Learning™

Christine Nasso, *Publisher*
Elizabeth Des Chenes, *Managing Editor*

© 2011 Greenhaven Press, a part of Gale, Cengage Learning

For more information, contact:

Greenhaven Press
27500 Drake Rd.
Farmington Hills, MI 48331-3535
Or you can visit our Internet site at
gale.cengage.com.

For product information and technology assistance, contact us at
Gale Customer Support, 1-800-877-4253.

For permission to use material from this text or product, submit all requests online at
www.cengage.com/permissions.

Further permissions questions can be e-mailed to
permissionrequest@cengage.com

Every effort is made to ensure that Greenhaven Press accurately reflects the original intent of the authors. Every effort has been made to trace the owners of copyrighted material.

Cover image © PhotoAlto/Alamy

LIBRARY OF CONGRESS CATALOGING-IN-PUBLICATION DATA

Henningfeld, Diane Andrews.
  Nature and wildlife / by Diane Andrews Henningfeld.
       p. cm. -- (Confronting global warming)
  Includes bibliographical references and index.
  ISBN 978-0-7377-5174-1 (hardcover)
  1. Nature conservation. 2. Wildlife conservation. 3. Nature--Effect of global warming on. 4. Wildlife--Effect of global warming on. I. Title.
    QH75.H3667 2011
    577.2'2--dc22
                                              2010038260

Printed in the United States of America
2 3 4 5 6 7 15 14 13 12 11

Contents

Preface

> *"The warnings about global warming have been extremely clear for a long time. We are facing a global climate crisis. It is deepening. We are entering a period of consequences."*
>
> *Al Gore*

Still hotly debated by some, human-induced global warming is now accepted in the scientific community. Earth's average yearly temperature is getting steadily warmer; sea levels are rising due to melting ice caps; and the resulting impact on ocean life, wildlife, and human life is already evident. The human-induced buildup of greenhouse gases in the atmosphere poses serious and diverse threats to life on earth. As scientists work to develop accurate models to predict the future impact of global warming, researchers, policy makers, and industry leaders are coming to terms with what can be done today to halt and reverse the human contributions to global climate change.

Each volume in the Confronting Global Warming series examines the current and impending challenges the planet faces because of global warming. Several titles focus on a particular aspect of life—such as weather, farming, health, or nature and wildlife—that has been altered by climate change. Consulting the works of leading experts in the field, Confronting Global Warming authors present the current status of those aspects as they have been affected by global warming, highlight key future challenges, examine potential solutions for dealing with the results of climate change, and address the pros and cons of imminent changes and challenges. Other volumes in the series—such as those dedicated to the role of government, the role of industry, and the role of the individual—address the impact various facets of society can have on climate change. The result is a series that provides students and general-interest readers with a solid understanding of the worldwide ramifications of climate change and what can be done to help humanity adapt to changing conditions and mitigate damage.

Each volume includes:

- A descriptive **table of contents** listing subtopics, charts, graphs, maps, and sidebars included in each chapter
- Full-color **charts, graphs, and maps** to illustrate key points, concepts, and theories
- Full-color **photos** that enhance textual material
- **Sidebars** that provide explanations of technical concepts or statistical information, present case studies to illustrate the international impact of global warming, or offer excerpts from primary and secondary documents
- **Pulled quotes** containing key points and statistical figures
- A **glossary** providing users with definitions of important terms
- An annotated **bibliography** of additional books, periodicals, and websites for further research
- A detailed **subject index** to allow users to quickly find the information they need

The Confronting Global Warming series provides students and general-interest readers with the information they need to understand the complex issue of climate change. Titles in the series offer users a well-rounded view of global warming, presented in an engaging format. Confronting Global Warming not only provides context for how society has dealt with climate change thus far but also encapsulates debates about how it will confront issues related to climate in the future.

Foreword

Earth's climate is a complex system of interacting natural components. These components include the atmosphere, the ocean, and the continental ice sheets. Living things on earth—or, the biosphere—also constitute an important component of the climate system.

Natural Factors Cause Some of Earth's Warming and Cooling

Numerous factors influence Earth's climate system, some of them natural. For example, the slow drift of continents that takes place over millions of years, a process known as plate tectonics, influences the composition of the atmosphere through its impact on volcanic activity and surface erosion. Another significant factor involves naturally occurring gases in the atmosphere, known as greenhouse gases, which have a warming influence on Earth's surface. Scientists have known about this warming effect for nearly two centuries: These gases absorb outgoing heat energy and direct it back toward the surface. In the absence of this natural greenhouse effect, Earth would be a frozen, and most likely lifeless, planet.

Another natural factor affecting Earth's climate—this one measured on timescales of several millennia—involves cyclical variations in the geometry of Earth's orbit around the sun. These variations alter the distribution of solar radiation over the surface of Earth and are responsible for the coming and going of the ice ages every one hundred thousand years or so. In addition, small variations in the brightness of the sun drive minor changes in Earth's surface temperature over decades and centuries. Explosive volcanic activity, such as the Mount Pinatubo eruption in the Philippines in 1991, also affects Earth's climate. These eruptions inject highly reflective particles called aerosol into the upper part of the atmosphere, known as the stratosphere, where they can reside for a year or longer. These particles reflect some of the incoming sunlight back into space and cool Earth's surface for years at a time.

Human Progress Puts Pressure on Natural Climate Patterns

Since the dawn of the industrial revolution some two centuries ago, however, humans have become the principal drivers of climate change. The burning of fossil fuels—such as oil, coal, and natural gas—has led to an increase in atmospheric levels of carbon dioxide, a powerful greenhouse gas. And farming practices have led to increased atmospheric levels of methane, another potent greenhouse gas. If humanity continues such activities at the current rate through the end of this century, the concentrations of greenhouse gases in the atmosphere will be higher than they have been for tens of millions of years. It is the unprecedented rate at which we are amplifying the greenhouse effect, warming Earth's surface, and modifying our climate that causes scientists so much concern.

The Role of Scientists in Climate Observation and Projection

Scientists study Earth's climate not just from observation but also from a theoretical perspective. Modern-day climate models successfully reproduce the key features of Earth's climate, including the variations in wind patterns around the globe, the major ocean current systems such as the Gulf Stream, and the seasonal changes in temperature and rainfall associated with Earth's annual revolution around the sun. The models also reproduce some of the more complex natural oscillations of the climate system. Just as the atmosphere displays random day-to-day variability that we term "weather," the climate system produces its own random variations, on timescales of years. One important example is the phenomenon called El Niño, a periodic warming of the eastern tropical Pacific Ocean surface that influences seasonal patterns of temperature and rainfall around the globe. The ability to use models to reproduce the climate's complicated natural oscillatory behavior gives scientists increased confidence that these models are up to the task of mimicking the climate system's response to human impacts.

To that end, scientists have subjected climate models to a number of rigorous tests of their reliability. James Hansen of the NASA Goddard Institute for Space Studies performed a famous experiment back in 1988, when he subjected a climate model (one relatively primitive by modern standards) to possible future fossil fuel emissions scenarios. For the scenario that most closely matches actual emissions since then, the model's predicted course of global temperature increase shows an uncanny correspondence to the actual increase in temperature over the intervening two decades. When Mount Pinatubo erupted in the Philippines in 1991, Hansen performed another famous experiment. Before the volcanic aerosol had an opportunity to influence the climate (it takes several months to spread globally throughout the atmosphere), he took the same climate model and subjected it to the estimated atmospheric aerosol distribution. Over the next two years, actual global average surface temperatures proceeded to cool a little less than 1°C (1.8°F), just as Hansen's model predicted they would.

Given that there is good reason to trust the models, scientists can use them to answer important questions about climate change. One such question weighs the human factors against the natural factors to determine responsibility for the dramatic changes currently taking place in our climate. When driven by natural factors alone, climate models do not reproduce the observed warming of the past century. Only when these models are also driven by human factors—primarily, the increase in greenhouse gas concentrations—do they reproduce the observed warming. Of course, the models are not used just to look at the past. To make projections of future climate change, climate scientists consider various possible scenarios or pathways of future human activity.

The earth has warmed roughly 1°C since preindustrial times. In the "business as usual" scenario, where we continue the current course of burning fossil fuel through the twenty-first century, models predict an additional warming anywhere from roughly 2°C to 5°C (3.6°F to 9°F). The models also show that even if we were to stop fossil fuel burning today, we are probably committed to as much as 0.6°C additional warming because of the inertia of the climate system. This inertia ensures warming for a century to come, simply due to our greenhouse gas emissions thus far. This committed warming introduces a profound procrastination penalty for not taking immediate action. If we are to avert an additional warming of 1°C, which would bring the net warming to 2°C—often considered an appropriate threshold for defining dangerous human impact on our climate—we have to act almost immediately.

Long-Term Warming May Bring About Extreme Changes Worldwide

In the "business as usual" emissions scenario, climate change will have an array of substantial impacts on our society and the environment by the end of this century. Patterns of rainfall and drought are projected to shift in such a way that some regions currently stressed for water resources, such as the desert southwest of the United States and the Middle East, are likely to become drier. More intense rainfall events in other regions, such as Europe and the midwestern United States, could lead to increased flooding. Heat waves like the one in Europe in summer 2003, which killed more than thirty thousand people, are projected to become far more common. Atlantic hurricanes are likely to reach greater intensities, potentially doing far more damage to coastal infrastructure.

Furthermore, regions such as the Arctic are expected to warm faster than the rest of the globe. Disappearing Arctic sea ice already threatens wildlife, including polar bears and walruses. Given another 2°C warming (3.6°F), a substantial portion of the

Greenland ice sheet is likely to melt. This event, combined with other factors, could lead to more than 1 meter (about 3 feet) of sea-level rise by the end of the century. Such a rise in sea level would threaten many American East Coast and Gulf Coast cities, as well as low-lying coastal regions and islands around the world. Food production in tropical regions, already insufficient to meet the needs of some populations, will probably decrease with future warming. The incidence of infectious disease is expected to increase in higher elevations and in latitudes with warming temperatures. In short, the impacts of future climate change are likely to have a devastating impact on society and our environment in the absence of intervention.

Strategies for Confronting Climate Change

Options for dealing with the threats of climate change include both adaptation to inevitable changes and mitigation, or lessening, of those changes that we can still affect. One possible adaptation would be to adjust our agricultural practices to the changing regional patterns of temperature and rainfall. Another would be to build coastal defenses against the inundation from sea-level rise. Only mitigation, however, can prevent the most threatening changes. One means of mitigation that has been given much recent attention is geoengineering. This method involves perturbing the climate system in such a way as to partly or fully offset the warming impact of rising greenhouse gas concentrations. One geoengineering approach involves periodically shooting aerosol particles, similar to ones produced by volcanic eruptions, into the stratosphere—essentially emulating the cooling impact of a major volcanic eruption on an ongoing basis. As with nearly all geoengineering proposals, there are potential perils with this scheme, including an increased tendency for continental drought and the acceleration of stratospheric ozone depletion.

The only foolproof strategy for climate change mitigation is the decrease of greenhouse gas emissions. If we are to avert a dangerous 2°C increase relative to preindustrial times, we will probably need to bring greenhouse gas emissions to a peak within the coming years and reduce them well below current levels within the coming decades. Any strategy for such a reduction of emissions must be international and multipronged, involving greater conservation of energy resources; a shift toward alternative, carbon-free sources of energy; and a coordinated set of governmental policies that encourage responsible corporate and individual practices. Some contrarian voices argue that we cannot afford to take such steps. Actually, given the procrastination penalty of not acting on the climate change problem, what we truly cannot afford is to delay action.

Evidently, the problem of climate change crosses multiple disciplinary boundaries and involves the physical, biological, and social sciences. As an issue facing all of civilization, climate change demands political, economic, and ethical considerations. With the Confronting Global Warming series, Greenhaven Press addresses all of these considerations in an accessible format. In ten thorough volumes, the series covers the full range of climate change impacts (water and ice; extreme weather; population, resources, and conflict; nature and wildlife; farming and food supply; health and disease) and the various essential components of any solution to the climate change problem (energy production and alternative energy; the role of government; the role of industry; and the role of the individual). It is my hope and expectation that this series will become a useful resource for anyone who is curious about not only the nature of the problem but also about what we can do to solve it.

Michael E. Mann

Michael E. Mann is a professor in the Department of Meteorology at Penn State University and director of the Penn State Earth System Science Center. In 2002 he was selected as one of the fifty lead-

ing visionaries in science and technology by Scientific American. *He was a lead author for the "Observed Climate Variability and Change" chapter of the Intergovernmental Panel on Climate Change (IPCC) Third Scientific Assessment Report, and in 2007 he shared the Nobel Peace Prize with other IPCC authors. He is the author of more than 120 peer-reviewed publications, and he recently coauthored the book* Dire Predictions: Understanding Global Warming *with colleague Lee Kump. Mann is also a co-founder and avid contributor to the award-winning science web-site RealClimate.org.*

CHAPTER 1

Global Warming, Nature and Wildlife: An Overview

Global warming has been the topic of intense scientific study, political debate, and news coverage over the past decades. Several essential questions emerge from the controversy: Is the earth warming? Is global warming part of a natural cycle or have humans caused it? Most importantly, how will global warming affect all the flora and fauna of the earth? Will people, wildlife, and plants be able to adapt to a changing climate?

Scientists Search for Facts

Many people look to science to offer answers to these questions. Scientists are, through their training and nature, by and large skeptical. They draw conclusions only when the conclusions can be supported by empirical, observable evidence. They do not accept a hypothesis as true until there is nearly overwhelming supporting data. Even then, if new evidence arises that contradicts or calls into question an established theory or hypothesis, scientists will modify or change their conclusions to fit the facts.

Scientists, using observable data and computer modeling, are nearly uniform in the conclusion that the earth's climate is changing rapidly. In addition, most scientists also believe that the changes are largely anthropogenic, that is, caused by humans through the burning of fossil fuels and other actions that increase the amount of greenhouse gases in the atmosphere.

Global Warming as a Natural Process

Global warming, however, begins with a natural process: sunlight hitting the earth. The sunlight warms the land, air, and ocean. Without this warmth, life on the earth would be impossible. The warmed earth reflects heat back into space in the form of infrared light. Greenhouse gases such as carbon dioxide (CO_2), water vapor, atmospheric methane, nitrous oxide, and ozone, circulating in the upper atmosphere, trap infrared radiation and reflect it back toward the earth, however. This is part of a natural cycle that makes the earth so hospitable to life; without the greenhouse gases, according to the National Aeronautics and Space Administration (NASA), the earth's average temperature would be only 0°F (-18°C). The problem, however, is that humans have been flooding the atmosphere with greenhouse gases for about the last 250 years, at an ever-increasing rate. These gases make it difficult for thermal radiation to escape the earth's atmosphere, and they lead to greater warming. Thus, while the warming of the earth is a natural process, global warming and climate change due to the rapid increase of greenhouse gases is, according to most scientists, something humans have created.

Climate-Change Deniers

Individuals who deny that the climate is changing, or who argue that the climate may be changing but that humans have little, if anything, to do with the change, have received a good deal of attention from the media. Indeed, there is evidence that the attention climate-change deniers have received has swayed American attitudes toward global warming. Gallup Poll editor-in-chief Frank Newport summarizes the results of a 2010 poll:

> Americans' attitudes toward the environment show a public that over the last two years has become less worried about the threat of global warming, less convinced that its effects are already happening, and more likely to believe that scientists themselves are uncertain about its occurrence.[1]

It is essential, however, when forming ideas about the causes and effects of global climate change to be as skeptical as a scientist: On what basis do climate change deniers make their claims? NASA space scientist David Morrison, writing in the *Skeptical Inquirer*, argues, "One of the goals of the deniers seems to be to sow confusion and give the impression that the science behind global warming is weak. . . . Most of the counterarguments don't make scientific sense, or else they are based on information that is obsolete." After noting that scientists have been in agreement about global warming for more than a decade, Morrison warns readers, "It is fine to be skeptical, but we need to be concerned when skepticism drifts into denial."[2]

What Scientific Evidence Reveals

There are many good reasons most scientists believe that the earth is in the midst of global warming. Observable data reveals that average global temperatures have risen between 1.08°F and 1.62°F (0.6°C and 0.9°C) over the past 100 years, according to Holli Riebeek, writing in NASA's *Earth Observatory*. In addition, Riebeek reports, "The rate of warming in the last 50 years was double the rate observed over the last 100 years," suggesting that the rate of change is escalating dramatically.[3]

Not only are average temperatures increasing, there is an even greater increase in extreme temperatures. According to the Pew Center on Global Climate Change, "In recent decades, hot days and nights have grown more frequent and cold days and nights less frequent. There have been more frequent heat waves and hotter high temperature extremes."[4]

The effects of global warming are much more profound than simply a rise in average temperatures or the increase in heat waves. Scientists have also recorded a trend toward earlier springs and later winters. Changes in seasonality dramatically affect nature, wildlife, and the ecosystems of which they are a part. In addition, severe weather events such as hurricanes and floods are increasing in both severity and frequency. The shift toward a

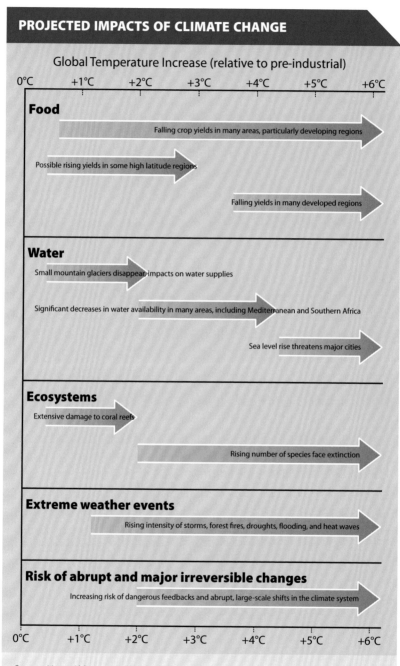

PROJECTED IMPACTS OF CLIMATE CHANGE

Global Temperature Increase (relative to pre-industrial)

0°C +1°C +2°C +3°C +4°C +5°C +6°C

Food

Falling crop yields in many areas, particularly developing regions

Possible rising yields in some high latitude regions

Falling yields in many developed regions

Water

Small mountain glaciers disappear, impacts on water supplies

Significant decreases in water availability in many areas, including Mediterranean and Southern Africa

Sea level rise threatens major cities

Ecosystems

Extensive damage to coral reefs

Rising number of species face extinction

Extreme weather events

Rising intensity of storms, forest fires, droughts, flooding, and heat waves

Risk of abrupt and major irreversible changes

Increasing risk of dangerous feedbacks and abrupt, large-scale shifts in the climate system

0°C +1°C +2°C +3°C +4°C +5°C +6°C

Source: Hugo Ahlenius, Nordphil, UNEP/GRID-Arendal, 2009. maps.grida.no/go/graphic/projected-impacts-of-climate-change. Source data taken from *Stern Review*, 2008.

warmer climate is also leading to ice melt flowing from the polar ice caps and from mountain glaciers that affects the flora and fauna living in these ecosystems. The Intergovernmental Panel on Climate Change (IPCC) noted in its 2007 report that snow and ice have been declining for many years, especially since 1980. In addition, the IPCC reports, "Most mountain glaciers are getting smaller. Snow cover is retreating earlier in the spring. Sea ice in the Arctic is shrinking in all seasons, most dramatically in the summer."[5] As a result of glacial melting, ocean levels are rising, and the IPCC predicts that the rate of ocean-level rise will increase in the coming years.

The Relationship Between Global Warming and Wildlife and Nature

Trying to determine how global warming is affecting wildlife and nature is a complicated matter; it is nearly impossible to sort out what can be attributed to climate change and what can be attributed to other factors. As London-based zoologists Karina Acevedo-Whitehouse and Amanda L.J. Duffus suggest, "Predicting the consequences of global environmental change on biodiversity is a complex task mainly because the effects encompass multiple and dynamic processes that rarely have single and clear-cut actions."[6] For example, human overpopulation can lead to the loss of wildlife habitat. So, too, can desertification caused by global warming, however. In an area with a growing human population that is trying to live on less and less arable land, wildlife can be forced out of its habitat. Is the culprit, in this instance, global warming or human overpopulation?

Moreover, climate change introduces a host of synergistic processes. That is, each factor builds on and exacerbates other factors. All are interrelated, and many are made worse because of the interrelationship. For example, human agricultural practices can lead to wildfires that destroy habitat and wildlife. Rising temperatures and the increasing number of droughts caused by global warming also increase the risk of wildfire, however.

When these two factors interact, the risk of wildfire increases dramatically, a risk greater than the one associated with either factor alone. Therefore, when examining the effects of climate change on wildlife and nature, it is important to consider how these effects interact with other conditions that may or may not be caused by global warming.

One thing is certain, however: Nature and wildlife are being changed as a result of global warming. As biologist Terry L. Root and climatologist Stephen H. Schneider write,

> Animals are showing many different types of changes related to climate. These include changes in ranges; abundances; phenology (timing of an event); morphology and physiology; and community composition, biotic interactions, and behavior. Changes are being seen in all different types of taxa, from insects to mammals, and on many of the continents.

Habitat Loss

Climate change affects flora and fauna habitats in numerous ways: drought, flood, wildfire, desertification, eutrophication, ice melt, and sea-level rise. Indeed, Root and Schneider argue, "The synergistic, or combined, effects of habitat fragmentation and climate change represent one of the most potentially serious global change problems."[7]

Drought, for example, kills off plants and trees necessary for animal survival, as does wildfire, a common companion to drought. Desertification, the gradual change of land that can support plant growth and life to nonarable land, is also the result of drought and rising temperatures. Likewise, flood stemming from the extreme rain events predicted by global warming models wipes out animal habitats. Habitat fragmentation and loss is also caused by human interaction with the ecosystem. Farmers looking to expand acreage for crops, for example, may cut down forests or engage in poor farming practices that reduce habitat, either of which can leave the land open for further damage from the effects of global warming.

Forests, wetlands, grasslands, lakes, rivers, reefs, and the ocean: Nature's great variety provides habitats for creatures great and small, as well as an abundance of plant life. In each case, though, climate change, combined with other exacerbating factors, is increasing the loss of habitat for flora and fauna. When habitats become too fragmented, wildlife populations become isolated and face the dangers of steep decline and extinction.

Emerging Wildlife and Plant Diseases

Just as global warming is predicted to affect human health in a variety of ways, rapid climate change is already having an impact on the health of wildlife and plants. Both plants and wildlife are encountering a whole host of new pathogens directly or indirectly connected to a warming planet. Many fungi, molds, bacteria, viruses, and insect pests are becoming more common or are expanding range because the climate is changing in ways that favor their hardiness and their expansion. For example, the National Wildlife Federation asserts that warmer air and water in such places as the Chesapeake Bay will contribute to harmful algal blooms, increase the size of dead zones, and encourage marine diseases.

Likewise, tree pests such as the hemlock wooly adelgid will be able to survive warmer winters, whereas in the past, the severe winters in the northern United States have limited its impact and range to the south. Many trees are likely to be lost to this insect pest.

Amphibians in particular are already showing signs of stress that stems from a combination of factors, including climate change. Scientists previously believed, for example, that the extinction of the golden toad of Costa Rica could be attributed to climate change. Research and observation have led scientists to

Following page: Tree pests such as the hemlock wooly adelgid—seen here attacking a hemlock pine tree in Chimney Rock, N.C.—can survive milder winters and therefore cause more damage to trees. AP Images/Chuck Burton.

the conclusion that the more likely cause of the toad's demise was the chytrid fungus. Scientists also note, however, that the fungus began its devastation of the golden toads during a particularly dry and hot period, conditions that are likely to become more common with global warming. Thus, while global warming might not be the primary cause of an increase in some diseases, it is a contributory influence in many such diseases.

Animal Immunity and Reproduction

Another cause for concern is the impact of climate change on animal immune and reproductive systems. The conditions of global warming, including drought, high temperatures, and extreme weather, stress the flora and fauna in any ecosystem. Stress caused by dehydration and malnutrition brought on by drought makes an organism more vulnerable to opportunistic diseases. An animal's immune system can be suppressed in such cases.

Likewise, stress can prevent or impair a species' ability to reproduce. In times of limited resources, many species forgo breeding. Individuals that do breed find it difficult to provide for their young, and such offspring might not survive.

Biologist and program director of the Wildlife Habitat Council Raissa Marks notes that conditions associated with global warming, such as higher temperatures and less moisture, affects amphibian and reptile populations, for example. She writes, "These climate changes can mean fewer insects available as prey for some species, changes in activity patterns, depressed immune systems due to stress, and shorter breeding seasons because ponds hold less water for shorter periods."[8] Moreover, she notes, nest temperatures affect the sex ratio of amphibian and reptile offspring. In optimal temperatures, there is about an even number of male and female offspring. In warmer temperatures, however, some species produce more male offspring while other species produce more female. In both cases, higher nest temperatures result in an imbalance between the number of males and females.

The breeding habits of migrating birds are also likely to be seriously affected by climate change. In the northern Midwest of the United States, small, temporary ponds called prairie potholes provide important breeding grounds. Changes in seasonality, spring arriving early, and rising temperatures can together cause the potholes to dry up before the birds have fledged their young, thus damaging the chances for survival of both young and adult birds, as well as placing entire species in danger.

Global Warming and Water Quality

Water is essential for all life on the planet. Rivers, streams, lakes, wetlands, and the ocean provide nutrition and shelter for a wide variety of plants and wildlife. As the climate changes, however, the quality of water is also changing, affecting those plants and animals that depend directly on the ocean or freshwater for survival.

Rising ocean temperatures, for example, cause marine organisms to experience stress in several ways. According to ecologists Kevin D. Lafferty, James W. Porter, and Susan E. Ford, in tropical waters, the water temperature is already near the lethal level for many organisms. Any warming at all will kill off these organisms. In addition, an increase in water temperature causes a decrease in oxygen. Therefore, marine organisms must work harder to get the oxygen they need from the water, increasing their metabolism. In some places, the ocean has been depleted of all its usable oxygen, creating so-called dead zones where neither plants nor animals can exist. These areas are expanding as the climate warms.

Another problem with water quality is increasing salinity in coastal freshwater resources. This change occurs because ocean levels are rising at the same time that severe weather is increasing. A storm surge from the ocean can flood coastal plains with saltwater, polluting wetlands, lakes, rivers, and ponds. Organisms that live in freshwater are often unable to survive in saltwater.

The Dangers of Ocean Acidification

The increased level of the greenhouse gas CO_2 is also causing acidification of the ocean, as evidenced by changing pH levels in ocean water. The increased acidity of the ocean destroys coral, mollusks, and any calcareous organisms (organisms that have shells or structures made from calcium carbonate). This condition is dangerous for the entire oceanic ecosystem. Acidification threatens to destroy diatoms and foraminifera, single-celled planktonic organisms that are the basis of the ocean's food chain. The destruction of plankton could lead to the collapse of the entire nutritional structure in some regions of the ocean. The British Royal Society reported on July 6, 2009, that "[coral] reefs are likely to be the first major planetary-scale ecosystem to collapse in the face of climate changes now in progress." The Royal Society extended its warning to all carbonate-dependent organisms as well, stating,

> The effects of ocean acidification will directly impact all carbonate dependent taxa: not only corals, but calcareous algae, most mollusks, many crustaceans, echinoderms and planktonic taxa, and other groups that rely on carbonates for skeletal growth. This includes fish . . . and also the pelagic ecosystem of the Southern Ocean.[9]

Such grim predictions suggest that the earth is headed for a new age of extinctions, with many causes and fueled by global warming.

The Sixth Mass Extinction

Scientists have evidence that the earth has gone through five major extinction events in its history. Many now argue that the earth is entering the sixth major extinction event. A combination of factors is causing many species to die out: loss of habitat, immune and reproductive failures, emerging diseases, human incursion into wild areas, pollution, and climate change. When these separate factors work together synergistically, many plants

Climate Change and the "Evil Quartet"

In a famous synopsis of the sources of human caused extinction, [biologist Jared] Diamond defined the evil quartet of drivers: overkill, habitat destruction, introduced species and chains of extinctions. Later work underscored the point that most extinctions involved a synergy of these factors with individual causes being difficult or impossible to isolate. We must now add severe anthropogenic interference with the global climate system to this list. . . . A clear lesson from the past is that the faster and more severe the rate of global change, the more devastating the biological consequences.

Compounding the problems associated with the rate of recent climate change is that species trying to shift distribution to keep pace must now contend with heavily modified landscapes dominated by agriculture, roads and urban development. . . . The new bioclimatic conditions and altered composition of ecological communities might also facilitate invasions by non-indigenous species that act as novel competitors or predators to stress resident species further. Harvest, habitat modification and altered fire regimes will also interact with, and probably enhance the direct impacts of climate change.

SOURCE: Barry W. Brook, Navjot S. Sodhi, and Corey J.A. Bradshaw, "Synergies Among Extinction Drivers Under Global Change," *Trends in Ecology & Evolution*, vol. 23, no. 8, August 2008, p. 459.

and much wildlife are in grave danger. The rate of extinction is steadily increasing, and biodiversity is diminishing. Scientists predict that many mammals will die out in the coming years.

In addition, scientists also point to the problem of coextinctions, when species that depend on each other go extinct simultaneously. Such events create a cascading effect, causing additional endangerments and extinctions. For example, when an animal that is low on the food chain becomes scarce or extinct, it puts pressure on predators higher on the food chain to find food. These predators may not be able to find food that meets their nutritional needs, which leads to malnutrition, suppressed immunity, failure to reproduce, and ultimately death. Another example can be found among organisms that exist in symbiosis, in which one organism depends on the other for survival. Corals and algae live in such a symbiotic relationship. When the algae die off, the coral follows. One cannot survive without the other. Consequently, when one partner in a symbiotic relationship becomes extinct, so, too, will the other partner.

Life is a complex web, one that includes fungi and the enormous blue whales, a single bacterium and the giant redwoods.

Life on Earth: The Importance of Biodiversity

Biodiversity encompasses all of life on the planet, in all its wonderful variety. The United Nations Secretariat of the Convention on Biological Diversity estimates that 1.75 million species have been identified but notes that scientists believe at least 13 million species exist. Biodiversity is important for many reasons: The interplay of all the earth's organisms creates a world that can support and sustain life. Life is a complex web, one that includes fungi and the enormous blue whales, a single bacterium and the giant redwoods. The diversity of life is created by genetic differences. When species become extinct, their genetic codes are lost to the world. Genetic richness is important for all of the creatures of the earth.

In addition, many medicines, foods, and other important attributes of plants and animals have not even been discovered yet. Who knows what is lost when a plant species is completely destroyed through slash-and-burn agriculture or through drought made worse by global warming? As the UN Convention argues,

"The loss of biodiversity threatens our food supplies, opportunities for recreation and tourism, and sources of wood, medicines, and energy. It also interferes with ecological functions."[10]

Global warming, in concert with other anthropogenic factors such as pollution and habitat degradation, threatens global biodiversity. In many cases, research that focuses on nature and wildlife provides the very clues needed in understanding the long-range implications of climate change as well as adaptations humans can make to help prevent extinctions and preserve biodiversity.

Notes

1. Frank Newport, "Americans' Global Warming Concerns Continue to Drop. Multiple Indicators Show Less Concern, More Feelings That Global Warming Is Exaggerated," Gallup Poll News Service, March 11, 2010. www.gallup.com.
2. David Morrison, "Disinformation About Global Warming: Most Arguments from Global Warming Disputers Don't Make Scientific Sense or Are Based on Distorted or Obsolete Information," *Skeptical Inquirer*, vol. 34, no. 2, March–April 2010, pp. 48–50.
3. Holli Riebeek, "Global Warming," *Earth Observatory*, May 11, 2007; updated April 26, 2010. earthobservatory.nasa.gov.
4. The Pew Center on Global Climate Change, "Climate Change 101: Science and Impacts," *Climate Change 101: Understanding and Responding to Global Climate Change*, January 2009. www.pewclimate.org.
5. International Panel on Climate Change, *Climate Change 2007: The Physical Science Basis. Contribution of Working Group I to the Fourth Assessment Report of the Intergovernmental Panel on Climate Change*, S. Solomon et al., eds., Cambridge, UK: Cambridge University Press, 2008.
6. Karina Acevedo-Whitehouse and Amanda L.J. Duffus, "Effects of Environmental Change on Wildlife Health," *Philosophical Transactions of the Royal Society: Biological Sciences*, vol. 364, November 27, 2009, p. 3429.
7. Terry L. Root and Stephen H. Schneider, "Climate Change: Overview and Implications for Wildlife," *Wildlife Responses to Climate Change*, Washington, DC: Island Press, 2002, p. 2.
8. Raissa Marks, "Amphibians and Reptiles," *Fish and Wildlife Habitat Management Leaflet*, no. 35, National Resources Conservation Service and Wildlife Habitat Council, February 2006, p. 4.
9. The Royal Society, "The Coral Reef Crisis: Scientific Justification for Critical CO_2 Thresholds Levels of <350ppm: Output of the Technical Working Group Meeting," July 6, 2009, p. 10.
10. Secretariat of the Convention on Biological Diversity, "Sustaining Life on Earth: How the Convention on Biological Diversity Promotes Nature and Human Well-Being," April 2000, p. 3.

CHAPTER 2

Shrinking Habitat: The Land

Probably the biggest problem facing nature and wildlife in the present is the shrinking, fragmentation, and disappearance of habitats. A habitat is the natural home of an animal, plant, or other organism; when a habitat changes, some organisms are able to adapt. Other organisms are unable to survive in conditions that differ from their natural habitats.

Habitats as Complicated Ecosystems

Habitats can be beautifully complicated ecosystems. For example, longleaf pine forests, once common in the southern United States, are "among the richest ecosystems in North America, rivaling tallgrass prairies and the ancient forests of the Pacific Northwest in the number of species it shelters," according to natural history and science writer Doreen Cubie.[1] She lists northern bobwhite quail, gopher tortoises, eastern indigo snakes, Bachman's sparrow, and many other species that live in the longleaf forests.

When scientists speak of habitat loss, they are referring to a set of events that causes a particular habitat to change to such an extent that the indigenous plants and animals can no longer survive there. For example, if a housing development is placed in a forested area, the habitat is lost to birds, mammals, plants, and other organisms. Likewise, if the average temperature of a habitat rises too much, although the land is still there and available, the habitat is nevertheless lost to those creatures requiring cooler temperatures.

Habitat fragmentation occurs when a previously continuous habitat is broken into two or more smaller parts, separated by nonhabitat. As wildlife biologists Alan B. Franklin, Barry R. Noon, and T. Luke George point out, however, habitat fragmentation is not like breaking a dinner plate into separate pieces. Rather, they argue, "Habitat fragmentation generally occurs through habitat loss; unlike the broken plate, the sum of the fragments is less than the whole. . . . Thus, fragmentation usually involves both a *reduction* in area and a *breaking* into pieces."[2] They further suggest that when a whole habitat is broken into smaller, noncontiguous fragments, the fragments may be of a lesser quality than the whole.

Causes of Habitat Loss and Fragmentation

There are numerous reasons behind the loss and fragmentation of land habitats, and none of them can be studied without reference to the others. Indeed, just as a habitat is a complex system of temperature, vegetation, food sources, predators, humidity, and water, among many features, the forces behind habitat loss also form a complicated web. This web becomes significantly more dangerous, however, when climate change and global warming are factors.

World wide, habitat loss and degradation (affecting 40% of species assessed) and harvesting (hunting or gathering for food, medicine, fuel, and materials, which affect 17%) are by far the main threats to mammals.

One of the most pressing drivers of habitat loss and fragmentation is human encroachment upon wild areas. For example, as the population of a country or region grows, people must find new places to live where they can support themselves and their children. Often this process leads to dwellings and farms being constructed on land that was previously unoccupied by humans and that supported abundant wildlife. Many species are affected by human encroachment upon habitat; mammals appear to be particularly vulnerable. Indeed, as biodiversity and conservation specialist Jan Schipper and his research partners report, "World wide, habitat loss and degradation (affecting 40% of species assessed) and harvesting (hunting or gathering for food, medicine, fuel, and materials, which affect 17%) are by far the main threats to mammals."[3]

Another driver of habitat loss and fragmentation is pollution of the land and air. Again, it is difficult to separate pollution from human encroachment; the two often move into an area together. Various kinds of pollution affect nature and wildlife: smoke from industry, nitrogen from agricultural fertilizers, toxic wastes from plastics and packaging, and many others. Biologists Karina Acevedo-Whitehouse and Amanda L.J. Duffus summarize the research thus: "Pollutants can alter habitat quality, reduce nutrient availability and encourage toxic algae blooms along the coastlines . . . all of which can indirectly affect the survival of sensitive species. . . . Environmental change is likely to seriously impair the viability of wildlife."[4]

Climate change is another important driver of habitat loss, and it interacts with both human encroachment and pollution to form a deadly triumvirate in habitat destruction and fragmentation. Environmental scientists Paul Opdam and Dirk Wascher have studied the synergistic interplay of climate change and habitat fragmentation as "key pressures on biodiversity."[5] Opdam and Wascher point out that in a cohesive habitat, populations can move to accommodate the changes wrought by warming temperatures. In landscapes dominated by human use, however, habitats may be fragmented to such an extent that a species cannot migrate to a more hospitable habitat. Thus, while human encroachment is the primary cause of habitat fragmentation, climate change places additional pressures on biodiversity. This

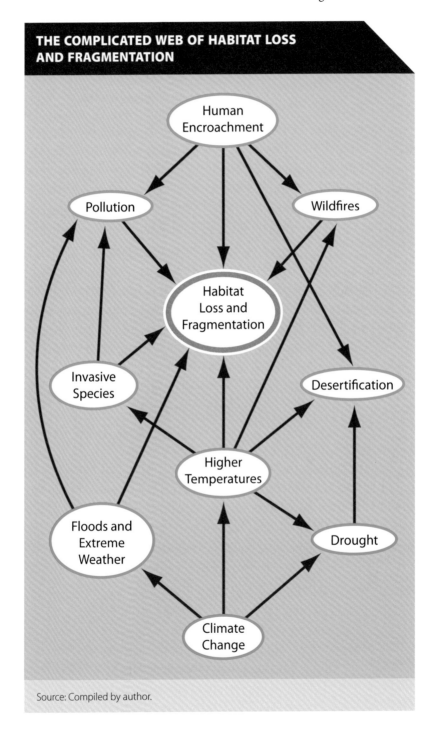

THE COMPLICATED WEB OF HABITAT LOSS AND FRAGMENTATION

Source: Compiled by author.

synergy directly and indirectly affects the conditions of a suitable habitat by imposing stress on the organisms that live there, sometimes to the point of extinction.

Requirements of a Suitable Habitat

A suitable habitat for a species requires particular types of vegetation, for nourishment, shelter, and sometimes for breeding purposes. Without the proper vegetation, wildlife will suffer from malnutrition or starvation. They may also be more vulnerable to predators, if they are not sheltered adequately by proper vegetation. Some species also require particular types of trees, bushes, or ground cover for nest building and rearing young.

In addition, a suitable habitat will have a stable range of temperatures in which the organism can sustain life. If temperatures are too hot for too long a period, organisms might suffer from heat prostration. If temperatures are too cold, organisms may freeze. Herpetofauna (a group name given to reptiles and amphibians), for example, are ectotherms. According to biologists Terry L. Root and Stephen H. Schneider, this designation means that the animals' "body temperatures adjust to the ambient temperature and radiation of the environment—they must avoid environments where temperatures are too cold or too hot."[6]

Finally, the availability of water is an important feature for a suitable habitat. Different species of plants and wildlife require greater or lesser amounts of water. Amphibians, for example, need water for reproduction. Root and Schneider note that amphibians must have wet habitats in order to keep their skins moist, as doing so is a means of respiration for them. Whereas amphibians are particularly dependent on water, all life on earth must have an adequate amount of water to sustain life.

The Effects of Drought on Habitat

Global warming is causing an increase in severe weather events, including droughts, excessive rain and flooding, violent storms, and heat waves and cold snaps. Severe weather can destroy

Habitat Loss and Severe Weather Endanger Copperbelly Snakes

Copperbelly water snakes migrate seasonally throughout their habitat, which consists of bottomland forests and shrub swamps. Although the species is [considered] a "water" snake, much of its time is spent away from water in the terrestrial, forested part of its habitat.

Copperbelly water snakes emerge from their hibernation sites in early spring and migrate through wooded or vegetated corridors to wetland areas. They can often be seen basking, breeding, and foraging near shallow wetland edges in woodlands. When the woodland swamps begin to dry in late spring or in early June, the snakes again disperse and move through wooded or vegetated corridors to their summer habitat areas. Summer activities usually center on forest and forest edges. For this reason, upland habitat is essential for the snake's summer foraging activities. By late fall, copperbelly water snakes seek out hibernation sites. . . .

Habitat loss and fragmentation [are] the primary causes of the decline of the copperbelly water snake and continue to be the major factors threatening the continued existence of the species. From 1790 to the mid-1980s, much of the copperbelly water snake's wetland habitat was modified or destroyed. By 1990, Indiana had lost 87% of its original wetlands, Illinois 85%, Michigan 50%, Ohio 90%, and Kentucky 81%. . . .

Weather extremes such as drought, flooding, and unusually mild, as well as severe, winters may influence the population of the copperbelly water snake. These factors affect the snake's ability to estivate for prolonged periods, as well as impeding access to, and use of, essential upland hibernation and foraging sites and wetland breeding areas. While these factors are not as likely to affect larger and healthier populations, small, isolated copperbelly water snake local clusters, like those that make up the northern population segment, are especially vulnerable to these naturally occurring events.

SOURCE: Walton Beacham, Frank V. Castronova, and Suzanne Sessine, eds., "Copperbelly Water Snake (*Nerodia erythrogaster neglecta*)," *Beacham's Guide to the Endangered Species of North America,* vol. 1, Detroit: Gale Group, 2001. http://galenet.galegroup.com.

vegetation, cause temperature extremes, and damage water supplies.

Drought is a long period of abnormally low rainfall. The Intergovernmental Panel on Climate Change reports, "As climate changes, several direct influences alter precipitation amount, intensity, frequency and type. Warming accelerates land surface drying and increases the potential incidence and severity of drought."[7] The Pew Center on Global Climate Change concurs, with an additionally worrisome note:

> Areas affected by drought are also expected to increase. As the atmosphere becomes warmer, it can hold more water, increasing the length of time between rain events and the amount of rainfall in an individual event. So, even areas where the average annual rainfall increases may experience more frequent and longer droughts.[8]

Often accompanied by high temperatures, drought can destroy habitats. Without adequate rainfall, vegetation that supplies food and shelter for a variety of species dies off.

Furthermore, during times of drought, plants and wildlife indigenous to the habitat can become stressed. Drought-resistant invasive species can capitalize on the weaknesses of indigenous species to overrun a habitat and effectively push out the organisms that had lived there previously.

Finally, drought can also lead to desertification, a process through which land that had been able to support life becomes increasingly dry and gradually turns to a desert that cannot sustain life. This process is occurring at present throughout the world, the results of global warming as well as poor agricultural methods. Furthermore, the process of desertification intensifies global warming. As the Asian Development Bank reports,

> Increased weather extremes such as droughts and heavy rains attributed to climate change as a result of global warming exacerbate the consequences of desertification while . . . the loss

of vegetation from desertification leads to increased carbon dioxide emissions and reduced carbon sink which in turn contributes to global warming.[9]

Excessive Rain, Floods, and Storms

In drought, habitats experience too little rainfall; drought is not the only extreme weather condition to destroy and fragment habitats, however. Ironically, as the Intergovernmental Panel on Climate Change (IPCC) notes, "The warmer climate . . . increases the risks of both drought—where it is not raining—and floods— where it is."[10] Sometimes a region or habitat will experience too much rainfall, leading to flooding of rivers, streams, and lakes. Not only do computer models predict excessive rain events for the future as a result of global warming, many areas of the world are already experiencing such downpours, as record levels of rain fall in short periods of time.

Flood can destroy habitats by killing everything in its path, including all kinds of wildlife and plants. In addition, floodwaters can carry with them toxic chemicals and heavy metals from industrial settings. When such contamination occurs, floodwaters affect the underlying soil and make regrowth difficult or impossible. Floods can completely upset or destroy the complicated relationships common in any ecosystem.

As the climate changes, according to the IPCC, violent storms are projected to increase in frequency and intensity. High winds, such as those found in tornadoes or hurricanes, destroy forest habitat and vegetation.

Temperature Extremes and Habitat

Temperature extremes negatively affect both flora and fauna. In general, organisms live in habitats that provide a range of temperatures within the lethal limits of an organism. That is, an animal will not live in a habitat that regularly grows so cold the animal freezes to death. Likewise, there is an upper temperature limit for most plants and animals, peculiar to each individual species. For example, reptiles and amphibians cannot tolerate extreme temperatures because they are cold-blooded creatures, meaning that the air temperature determines their body temperature. When the air is too hot, they die. When it is too cold, they die. Mammals are also confined to habitats that support their specific temperature requirements. For example, the green ringtail possums of Queensland, Australia, cannot tolerate temperatures above about 86°F (30°C).

Wildfires Destroy Habitats

As a result of human interference with forests and landscapes, as well as many parts of the world becoming hotter and drier, wildfires will become more common in time of global warming. Wildfires are very destructive to animals, plants, and their habitats. Fire destroys large swaths of trees, forests, and grasslands, home to many organisms. Although fires can be beneficial for some areas in nature in that they allow certain species of trees to propagate, in other cases wildfires destroy both wildlife and habitat.

In February 2009, for example, wildfires ripped through sections of Australia, following a ten-year-long drought and record high temperatures. Science writer Ken Eastwood relates that more than 1737 square miles (4500 sq. km) of bushland were destroyed in the fires. He writes, "Climatologists agree that it was climate change that made the February [2009] fires Australia's worst peacetime disaster."[11]

Furthermore, wildfires fragment habitat by destroying patches of land and making noncontiguous a habitat that was once connected. When this breaking apart happens, populations of wildlife and flora become isolated from one another.

Following page: A wildfire has damaged the habitat of this elk bull in Yellowstone National Park, Wyoming. Michael Quinton/Minden Pictures/Getty Images.

Population fragmentation is one of the drivers of extinction, and wildfires have the potential of pushing some endangered species over the brink.

Changes in the Climatic Envelope

The Australian Academy of Science defines a climatic envelope as the "range of temperatures, rainfall, and other climate-related parameters in which a species currently exists."[12] Global warming is causing significant change to the climatic envelope in many habitats. If a habitat becomes hotter and drier, for example, a species may migrate to a cooler, moister area. Thus, an animal living in a habitat that has become too hot, and too dry, might move its range to a higher altitude or away from the tropics and toward the poles (that is, northward in the northern hemisphere or southward in the southern hemisphere). The Audubon Society has documented northward shifts among North American bird populations, for example, during the past forty years for nearly every species of bird. The organization concludes, "Given the strong evidence that global warming is indeed a key factor in observed bird movements, shifts like these will continue for familiar species—for better or worse—as long as the climate continues to change."[13]

Some species, however, will be unable to migrate. As Root and Schneider observe, "Rapid movements by birds are possible because they can fly, but for herps [herpetofauna] such movements are much more difficult."[14] Thus, reptiles and amphibians are at special risk amid changing climatic conditions.

Human Encroachment and Invasive Species

Human encroachment—including roads, air routes, and cities— might also make it impossible for an animal to move. Some species may be able to adapt to living in the changed climatic conditions of their habitat. Others, however, will be unable to adapt, and they are likely to die off. For example, the mountain pygmy possum of Australia is doubly endangered: The loss of snow cover in the creature's habitat due to climate change negatively affects its hibernation patterns; and, at the same time, construction of ski resorts and human development in that habitat makes it difficult for the animals to move to a more hospitable climate. Likewise, some birds in the tropics are endangered by both human encroachment and the inability to move to a new habitat.

In addition to habitat loss and fragmentation from climate change, sometimes organisms lose their habitat to invasive species that are more adaptable to the changing climatic envelope. For example, in the Arctic, red foxes are displacing arctic foxes as the climate warms. Arctic foxes are being pushed farther and farther north as they lose the habitat to which they are best suited. Some animals, of course, will benefit from global warming. Wild Norwegian reindeer, for example, thrive in somewhat warmer temperatures and find their habitats expanding. In Canada, however, migratory woodland caribou, a subspecies closely related to Norwegian reindeer, are declining, largely because of their traditional habitat being lost to human interaction and the effects of global warming.

Notes

1. Doreen Cubie, "America's Forgotten Forest," *National Wildlife*, April 2, 2008. www.nwf.org.
2. Alan B. Franklin, Barry R. Noon, and T. Luke George, "What Is Habitat Fragmentation?" *Studies in Avian Biology*, vol. 25, 2002, p. 23.
3. Jan Schipper et al., "The Status of the World's Land and Marine Mammals: Diversity, Threat, and Knowledge," *Science*, vol. 322, October 10, 2008, p. 228.
4. Karina Acevedo-Whitehouse and Amanda L.J. Duffus, "Effects of Environmental Change on Wildlife Health," *Philosophical Transactions of the Royal Society: Biology*, vol. 364, November 27, 2009, p. 3429.
5. Paul Opdam and Dirk Wascher, "Climate Change Meets Habitat Fragmentation: Linking Landscape and Biogeographical Scale Levels in Research and Conservation," *Biological Conservation*, vol. 117, 2004, p. 285.
6. Terry L. Root and Stephen H. Schneider, "Climate Change: Overview and Implications for Wildlife," *Wildlife Responses to Climate Change: North American Case Studies*, Terry L. Root and Stephen H. Schneider, eds., Washington, DC: Island Press, 2002, p. 21.
7. International Panel on Climate Change, "How Is Precipitation Changing?" *Climate Change 2007: The Physical Science Basis: Contribution of Working Group I to the*

Fourth Assessment Report of the Intergovernmental Panel on Climate Change, S. Solomon et al., eds., Cambridge, UK: Cambridge University Press, 2007, p. 105.

8. The Pew Center on Global Climate Change, "Climate Change 101: Science and Impacts," *Climate Change 101: Understanding and Responding to Global Climate Change*, January 2009. www.pewclimate.org.

9. Asian Development Bank, "Combating Desertification in Asia," 2010. www.adb.org.

10. International Panel on Climate Change, "How Is Precipitation Changing?" p. 105.

11. Ken Eastwood, "Climate Change: The Smoking Gun in Australia's Firestorm," *Geographical*, vol. 81, no. 4, April 2009, pp. 20–21.

12. Australian Academy of Science, "Impact of Global Warming on Biodiversity," October 13, 2005. www.science.org.au.

13. National Audubon Society, "Birds and Climate Change: Ecological Disruption in Motion," February 2009. birdsandclimate.audubon.org.

14. Root, "Climate Change," p. 21.

CHAPTER 3

Shrinking Habitats: The Ocean, Ice, and Freshwater

Earth is a watery planet. Seventy percent of the earth's surface is covered with water, and every form of life, even life that has evolved in desert regions, requires water for survival. In addition, the mighty ocean, freshwater lakes, ponds, rivers, and streams are all important habitats for many species. Likewise, both sea ice and freshwater ice (for example, what is found in glaciers) support a variety of life forms. Just as the loss of land habitats is of grave concern to scientists, though, so too is the loss, fragmentation, and degradation of water habitats.

Causes of Water Habitat Loss

The loss of water habitats of all sorts can be attributed to many different causes, although human action is at the root of nearly all the degradation of water on the planet. Pollution is a huge problem, and it includes the damage done by oil spills, sewage overflow, and toxic chemical contamination. For centuries, the waters of the earth have been a convenient dumping ground for human waste and garbage. The advent of industry only made the problem of pollution much worse.

Likewise, anthropogenic global warming poses a serious and imminent threat to many watery habitats. Rising temperatures are warming the ocean, melting glaciers, and drying up freshwater. Furthermore, just as land habitats face damage from the indirect causes of global warming, such as severe weather events, water habitats likewise are vulnerable to such events as droughts, flooding, and storms.

Pollution, warming, severe weather: Together, these factors work synergistically to destroy habitats and the species that depend on those habitats, in both the short term and the long term. For example, species stressed by such contaminants in water as oil, heavy metals, or toxic chemicals are less likely to be able to contend with the demands placed on them by warmer water.

Warming Ocean

By far the earth's largest repository of water is its ocean. This saltwater body supports life in almost unimaginable variety, from giant whales to single-celled plankton. Evolutionary biologists believe that life on the planet first had its start in the prehistoric ocean. Moreover, the ocean absorbs CO_2, thus helping to reduce global warming. Indeed, the ocean is among its most important climatic features. According to N.L. Bindoff and Working Group I of the Intergovernmental Panel on Climate Change (IPCC), however, "The oceans are warming. Over the period 1961 to 2003, global ocean temperature has risen by 0.10°C from the surface to a depth of 700 m."[1] Although it might not seem to be a dramatic increase, the rate of warming is significant and is affecting the flora and fauna of the marine world.

Pollution, warming, severe weather: Together, these factors work synergistically to destroy habitats and the species that depend on those habitats, in both the short term and the long term.

Just as land species have specific requirements of their habitats in order to survive, so too do ocean species require a range of temperatures, nutrition, and shelter. There is observable evidence that the surface temperatures of the ocean are rising, however, and rising rapidly. Such warming can harm ocean ecosys-

Antarctica's Penguins

Penguins captured the hearts of moviegoers throughout the world with the 2005 film *March of the Penguins*, a French documentary tracing the daunting journeys taken by adult penguins each year in order to breed, birth, and feed their young. Since 1950, the population of emperor penguins in Adélie Coast, Antarctica, has been cut in half, according to Jon Roach, writing for *National Geographic News* in an article linking penguin decline to climate change. The complete story is complicated, however, and demonstrates ways that habitat loss, climate change, and human encroachment work together to endanger animals.

Although penguins spend a significant amount of their time swimming in water, solid sea ice is an essential component to the birds' habitat. Penguins breed, bear their young, and molt on sea ice. In addition, tiny crustaceans called krill depend for their survival on the algae that grow on the underside of sea ice. Krill is the penguins' primary food source. The loss of sea ice caused by warming temperatures and higher winds will, therefore, reduce the amount of food available for penguins and their young.

The warmer temperatures also mean that the penguins must rely upon ever-thinner ice on which to lay their eggs and protect their chicks. If the ice breaks apart before the chicks are old enough to swim, they will perish.

Not everyone believes, however, that the decline in the emperor penguin populations of Antarctica is due to global warming. Patrick J. Michaels, in his 2004 book *Meltdown: The Predictable Distortion of Global Warming by Scientists, Politicians and the Media* attributes penguin decline to the rapid growth of ecotourism to Antarctica. Viewing the birds during breeding season places stress on the creatures and changes their behavior. Other writers attribute penguin decline throughout the region to overfishing.

Once again, although it is difficult to tease out which of these forces is the most dangerous for penguins, it seems clear that the combined affect of warmer temperatures, human interference, and habitat loss are endangering the species.

tems, and it is doing so. As the warming increases, the damage cascades into catastrophic conditions for many species.

The Case of the Corals

An excellent example of such a cascade can be found in coral reefs. Coral reefs are formed by tiny organisms known as polyps that build calcium-based exoskeletons. Algae live symbiotically

Coral heads off the coast of Queensland, Australia, show evidence of bleaching due to stress in the environment. Ove Hoegh-Guidberg/AFP/Getty Images.

with coral; that is, the algae and the coral depend on each other for survival. Coral provides shelter for the algae, while algae produce nourishment for the coral through photosynthesis. The beautiful colors of coral reefs are not from the coral itself, but from the algae.

Coral can expel the algae if the rate of photosynthesis gets too high or if the coral becomes stressed, although generally coral and algae live together harmoniously. As the water temperature warms, however, coral begins to experience stress. As the water temperature continues to increase, coral begins to expel algae, leading to a phenomenon known as "bleaching," so-called because of the loss of color caused by algae expulsion. The National Oceanic and Atmospheric Administration reports, "Coral exposed to ocean temperatures of just 1.8 degrees Fahrenheit above average monthly temperatures frequently 'bleach' . . . by ejecting symbiotic algae that give the coral its color and help supply it with nutrients."[2] If the waters do not cool and the algae do not return, the coral dies from lack of nourishment.

An important point here is that during long-term, geologic changes in sea-surface temperatures, corals and algae have been able to adapt to slowly rising temperatures. The current trends in global warming, however, document a rapidly warming ocean, a change that is much too swift to allow organisms such as corals and algae to adapt.

Just as the ocean provides a habitat for coral, coral is the basis of a habitat that shelters and nourishes many other organisms, including fishes, plants, plankton, and other forms of life. Coral bleaching represents a violent destruction of a rich habitat. The plants and animals that depend on the coral habitat for survival must either find a new home or die. Global warming, therefore, puts into motion a cascade of events, beginning with coral bleaching and death, that leads to loss of habitat and death for other creatures low on the food chain; this outcome, in turn, leads to a loss of prey and food for creatures higher on the food chain.

The Arctic: Warmer Waters, Disappearing Sea Ice

Science writer Patrick Tucker asserts, "Many researchers argue that the rapid climatic and biota changes playing out in the Arctic provide a window to how temperatures and animal behaviors will shift as a result of climate change. The Arctic is warming about twice as fast as the rest of the planet."[3]

The warming of the ocean in the Arctic presents yet another example of habitat loss. For the past twenty to thirty years, roughly 17,374 square miles (45,000 sq. km) per year of sea ice has melted (sea ice is frozen ocean water, not to be confused with freshwater icebergs or glacier ice). R.K. Pachauri, chairman of the IPCC and director of Yale Climate and Energy Institute announced the "possible disappearance of sea ice by the latter part of the 21st century."[4] Although polar ice generally grows in the winter and recedes in the summer, during recent decades the sea ice has receded rapidly, leading some scientists to predict that within the next century, the Arctic may be ice free.

Arctic sea ice provides an important habitat for numerous birds and animals, including the ivory gull, the Pacific walrus, the ringed seal, and the hooded seal. The latter two are important prey species for another species, the polar bear, an animal that depends on sea ice for survival. The US Fish and Wildlife Service listed polar bears as a threatened species in 2008 under the US Endangered Species Act. The Polar Bear Study Group of the United Nations classified polar bears as "vulnerable" in 2005, and Russia calls polar bears a "species of concern." This widespread attention to the plight of polar bears and melting sea ice has opened a controversy over both the level of endangerment as well as the cause.

Polar Bear Populations: Conflicting Assertions

At present, estimates of polar bear populations range between 21,500 and 25,000 individuals, according to wildlife biologist Steven C. Amstrup in *Wild Mammals of North America* (2003).

The Polar Bear Specialist Group (PBSG) of the International Union for Conservation of Nature agrees with this statistic, noting that there are nineteen populations of bears. Of these, according to the PBSG, eight were declining, three were stable, and one was increasing. They were unable to determine the status of the remaining seven bands because of a lack of data.

According to many scientists, however, the plight of the polar bear is even more precarious than these numbers might suggest. Indeed, Polar Bears International argues, "As the Arctic continues to warm due to climate change, two-thirds of the world's polar bears could disappear by 2030."[5] Habitat loss and degradation caused by global warming are the major reasons behind this fear.

Sea ice is an important habitat feature for polar bears. As US Geologic Survey researcher Eric V. Regehr and his colleagues point out, "Polar bears depend on sea ice for movement and reproduction, as well as for hunting. . . . Extensive open water and increased ice roughness caused by the action of winter storms on thinner ice may reduce foraging success."[6] Regehr's team has determined that declines in the polar bear population can be associated with loss of ice. Furthermore, Regehr's research demonstrates that polar bears suffer nutritionally when sea ice is diminished. Thus, although many polar bears seem able to survive despite diminishing ice, they are malnourished and stressed as a result. Consequently, they may succumb to illness or starvation.

Nonetheless, not everyone agrees that polar bears are threatened, nor does everyone agree that polar bear endangerment can be attributed to global warming. There are individuals who believe that the polar bear has been selected as a "poster child" for global warming in order to promote a particular political agenda.

Kenneth Green, for example, argues, "At present, polar bear populations are robust and, according to native peoples living in the Arctic, are considerably larger than they were in previous de-

POLAR BEAR POPULATIONS

A Northern Beaufort Sea 980 (2007)	**F** Kane Basin 164 (1998)
B Viscount Melville 215 (1996)	**G** Gulf of Boothia 1,500 (2000)
C Norwegian Bay 190 (1998)	**H** Western Hudson Bay 935 (2004)
D Lancaster Sound 2,500 (1998)	**I** Southern Hudson Bay 1,000 (1988)
E McClintock Channel 284 (2000)	

PACIFIC
OCEAN

ARCTIC CIRCLE

Chukchi Sea
2,000+

Southern
Beaufort Sea
1,500
(2006)

CANADA

Laptev Sea
800–1,200
(1993)

Arctic Basin
Unknown

A

B

E

RUSSIA

H

NORTH POLE

Foxe
Basin
2,200
(1994)

G D C

F

Kara Sea
Unknown

Baffin
Bay
1,600
(2004)

I

Barents Sea
3,000
(2004)

Davis Strait
2,000
(2007)

GREENLAND

East Greenland
2,000+

ATLANTIC OCEAN

Source: Polar Bears International, *Population and Distribution Map*, 2010.
www.polarbearsinternational.org.

cades."[7] Green also contends that polar bears historically survived when temperatures were even warmer than in the present day.

Likewise, biologist Mitchell Taylor asserts, "There aren't just a few more bears. There are a lot more bears." Taylor is convinced that "threats to polar bears from global warming are exaggerated and that their numbers are increasing."[8] Taylor has studied polar bears for more than twenty years for the Nunavut government, a federal territory of Canada.

Both Green and Taylor have associations that also suggest particular political agendas. Ian Sample, writing in the February 2, 2007, issue of *The Guardian* notes that Green is a scholar with the American Enterprise Institute (AEI), a think tank largely funded by ExxonMobil, the large international oil company. Furthermore, the AEI sent letters to scientists offering to pay them up to $10,000 for articles that would discredit the Intergovernmental Panel on Climate Change, according to Sample, and confirmed by Green in *The Guardian*.[9] This connection provides context for Green's statement in *The American*: "If polar bears are placed on the endangered species list, the legal hurdles to oil and gas drilling will increase."[10]

Also, it is important to note that Taylor's studies have been commissioned and funded by the Nunavut government, according to Fred Langan and Tom Leonard writing in the March 9, 2007, issue of the *Telegraph*. Nunavut is the Inuit-dominated First Nation territory in Canada. According to Langan and Leonard, "Critics claim the government has an agenda to encourage polar bear hunting and keep the animals off the endangered species list."[11] Phred Dvorak, writing in *The Wall Street Journal*, notes additionally, "Sale of polar-bear skins for rugs and trophies accounts for the bulk of international trade in the bears. . . . Canadian Inuit groups say the loss of such sales . . . could be devastating for Arctic communities that have few sources of income."[12]

In sum, while the total population of polar bears remains in debate, clear-cut scientific evidence exists that polar bear populations decline with the increase of ice-free periods in areas of the Arctic. In addition, scientific evidence supports that ice-free periods in the Arctic are increasing and that the earth may be headed for a time when there is no ice in the Arctic Ocean. It seems clear, therefore, that if polar bears are dependent on sea ice, and if sea ice is melting at an unprecedented rate, then polar bears are threatened by a warmer future.

Rising Ocean Levels and Habitat Loss

Global warming models predict that ocean levels will rise as a consequence of the expansion of water caused by higher temperatures, and because of melting glaciers and land ice. Indeed, records show that the ocean has been rising for the past 100 years. That rate is expected to accelerate. The IPCC predicts that the average global sea level may rise as much as 23 inches (58 cm) over the next 100 years.

The National Oceanic and Atmospheric Administration (NOAA) asserts that a rise in sea level will cause habitat loss and destruction of shoreline ecosystems as the land falls beneath seawater. In addition, the rising ocean levels will cause a greater risk of flooding and storm surges from hurricanes and cyclones.

Seawater incursion resulting from flooding can destroy freshwater habitats located in rivers, ponds, and streams along coastlines, as freshwater organisms are not adapted to the salt content of seawater. Likewise, rising ocean levels will cause increased salinity in bays, sounds, and estuaries, making these habitats inhospitable for many species of plants and animals. NOAA states, "Due to existing shoreline development and protective structures (such as sea walls and bulkheads), wetlands, beaches and other intertidal areas many not be able to migrate inland as sea level rises. These important areas would drown under the rising sea."[13]

Finally, rising ocean levels will lead to coastal erosion. Creatures that make their homes along the shoreline risk habitat loss. Various birds and crustaceans that live in the shoreline ecosystem will have to adapt, move, or die. In some cases, islands may be completely inundated. Thus, creatures and plants living on such islands will be completely destroyed. *EarthTalk* sums up what rising ocean levels may mean for nature and wildlife thus:

> As for wildlife, it's unclear just how much certain endemic species will be affected by rising sea levels and other environmental hazards exacerbated by global warming. Clearly the biggest threat is habitat loss: Landforms that once sustained certain animals may no longer be above water or otherwise suitable for some species. Those fortunate to be on big continents may be able to move away from [the coast]. . . . But animals on islands may be hard pressed to find places better to go to where they can keep on keeping on.[14]

Freshwater Wetlands

Many species make their homes in freshwater wetlands such as swamps, marshes, fens, bogs, and tundra. According to the US Environmental Protection Agency, "Wetlands are areas where water covers the soil, or is present either at or near the surface of the soil all year, or for varying periods of time during the year, including during the growing season."[15] Depending on the soil, climate, vegetation, and a host of other factors, wetlands can take many different forms.

In some places wetlands are seasonal. For a part of the year, they have standing water and moisture; during other seasons they may be dry. This description is particularly fitting in more arid regions. The timing of when wetlands appear and how long they last is very important to the species that depend on them. In areas with declining rainfall, and in those areas experiencing drought, wetlands may vanish altogether or may become temporary. As ecologist W. Carter Johnson and his colleagues note, "Freshwater wetlands worldwide are projected to be particularly vulnerable to climate change. . . . Their shallow depths and rapid evaporation contribute most to this vulnerability."[16]

Many wetlands are experiencing abrupt and rapid climate change. This shift is due to increasing temperatures as well as changes in seasonality. In other words, spring is arriving earlier in some places, and winter is arriving later. These occurrences can change the hydrology of a wetland region and affect the mating and breeding of many species as well as the viability of their young.

Many wetland species, for example, require a minimum time of inundation to complete their life cycles. Migratory ducks, for example, need to find temporary wetlands such as those in the Prairie Pothole region of the upper Midwest of the United States at precisely the right time. W. Carter Johnson et al. note, "Early drying may be an ecological trap . . . whereby migrating ducks are attracted to wet basins in early spring but cannot fledge their young when wetlands dry up too quickly in the more evaporative greenhouse climate." They add that mallard ducklings' survival rate was 7.6 times lower during a drought period, and they conclude that climate change poses a serious "conservation challenge."[17]

Likewise, amphibians rely on the moisture found in wetland habitats for their survival. These animals may prove to have the most difficult time adjusting to climate change in that they cannot easily change their habitat, and they require significant water throughout the year for breeding, mating, nourishment, and health. Raissa Marks of the Wildlife Habitat Council writes, "Changes in climate, including higher temperatures, lower soil moisture, longer dry seasons and more variability in rainfall, can influence amphibian and reptile populations."[18] According to Marks, in addition to amphibians experiencing changes in their sources of food, the animals will also undergo "shorter breeding seasons because ponds hold less water for shorter periods."

Eutrophication

Habitats in small lakes and ponds are also suffering degradation and destruction from eutrophication. This process results from "nutrient overenrichment of waters by urban, agricultural, and industrial development" and leads to "the growth of cyanobacteria as harmful algal blooms," according to marine scientists Hans W.

Paerl and Jef Huisman.[19] In other words, overflows from sewage treatment, fertilizer runoff from farm fields, and waste products from industry can deposit too much nitrogen and other nutrients into a body of water. The water becomes a superrich soup in which harmful bacteria can thrive. Amid such conditions, the habitat of aquatic plants and fish is lost, and these species are often crowded out. Paerl and Huisman note that Lake Erie, one of the five Great Lakes, is an ecosystem threatened by eutrophication.

Although global warming is not the direct cause of eutrophication, it nonetheless exacerbates the process. As Paerl and Huisman report, warmer temperatures are better for cyanobacteria blooms for several reasons: Cyanobacteria grow better at increased temperatures; global warming causes water to stratify, which lengthens the potential growing season for the bacteria; and the bacteria float on the surface, shading the organisms growing deeper in the body of water. Thus, eutrophication has the potential to damage or destroy many freshwater habitats in a time of global warming.

Global Warming and Great Lakes Habitats

Lakes Superior, Huron, Michigan, Erie, and Ontario, known collectively as the Great Lakes of the United States, are the largest repositories of freshwater in the entire world. These lakes provide habitat for a wide array of plants and animals.

Computer models and scientists agree that it is likely that the Great Lakes region will grow warmer with climate change. The Great Lakes have experienced fluctuations in water levels throughout the time that records have been kept; extremely low water levels characterized the period from the mid-1990s through the first decade of the twenty-first century, however.

Projections by climatologists at the Environmental Protection Agency (EPA) indicate that increasing carbon dioxide levels will warm the Great Lakes basin by as much as 7°F (4°C). According to the EPA, "Warmer climates mean increased evaporation from the lake surface and evapotranspiration from the land surface of the basin. This in turn will augment the percentage of precipitation that is returned to the atmosphere. . . . The resulting decreases in average lake levels will be from half a meter to two meters."[20] It is possible that those plants and other organisms dwelling in the on-shore waters of the Great Lakes will find their habitats destroyed by the dropping lake levels.

Scientists also believe that winter ice cover will decline throughout the region. Biologists George Kling and Donald Wuebbles write that although loss of winter ice "may be a mixed blessing for fish, reducing winterkill in shallow lakes," this loss will seriously jeopardize the whitefish population of the Great Lakes. They note, "Ice cover protects [whitefish] eggs from winter storm disturbance."[21]

As the climate warms, some fish will move farther north, and there will be a significant redistribution of species throughout the Great Lakes. The stress on the ecosystem weakens the native plants and other indigenous species, however, making it easier for invasive species to crowd them out.

Finally, it is likely that summer stratification of the lake waters will increase and last longer, with warmer water staying on the surface of the lake. This condition means that the turnover of water that generally takes place in the spring and fall may be decreased. Kling and Wuebbles assert, "In all lakes, the duration of summer stratification will increase, adding to the risk of oxygen depletion and formation of deep-water 'dead zones' for fish and other organisms." Thus, climate change stands to transform the Great Lakes from an ecosystem that teems with life to one that cannot support life at all. Those organisms that inhabit the lakes will find their habitats lost, fragmented, or so degraded that they will not be able to survive.

Notes

1. N.L. Bindoff et al., "2007: Observations: Oceanic Climate Change and Sea Level," *Climate Change 2007: The Physical Science Basis. Contribution of Working Group I to the Fourth Assessment Report of the Intergovernmental Panel on Climate Change*, S. Solomon et al., eds., Cambridge, UK: Cambridge University Press, 2007, p. 387.

2. National Oceanic and Atmospheric Administration (NOAA), Ocean and Coastal Resource Management, "Climate Change," October 6, 2009. www.coastalmanage mentnoaa.gov.

3. Patrick Tucker, "Arctic Species at the Cliff's Edge: New Paper Models Changes for Arctic Species Due to Climate Change," *The Futurist*, vol. 44, no. 1, January–February 2010, p. 8.

4. R.K. Pachauri, UN Summit on Climate Change, September 22, 2009. www.ipcc.ch.

5. Polar Bears International, "FAQs About Polar Bears," 2010, www.polarbearsinter national.org.

6. Eric V. Regehr et al., "Survival and Breeding of Polar Bears in the Southern Beaufort Sea in Relation to Sea Ice," *Journal of Animal Ecology*, vol. 79, 2010, pp. 123–24.

7. Kenneth Green, "Are Polar Bears Really an Endangered Species?" *The American*, May 13, 2008. www.american.com.

8. Quoted in Fred Langan, "Canadian Controversy: How Do Polar Bears Fare?" *Christian Science Monitor*, May 3, 2007. www.csmonitor.com.

9. Ian Sample, "Scientists Offered Cash to Dispute Climate Study," *The Guardian*, February 2, 2007. www.guardian.co.uk.

10. Green, "Are Polar Bears Really an Endangered Species?" *The American*, May 13, 2008. www.american.com.

11. Fred Langan and Tom Leonard, "Polar Bears 'Thriving as the Arctic Warms Up,'" *The Telegraph*, March 9, 2007. www.telegraph.com.uk.

12. Phred Dvorak, "The Hunt for a Clear Picture of Polar Bears' Future," *Wall Street Journal*, January 7, 2010.

13. NOAA, "Climate Change."

14. *EarthTalk: Questions & Answers About Our Environment*, January 10, 2010. www .emagazine.com.

15. US Environmental Protection Agency, "What Are Wetlands?" January 12, 2009. www .epa.gov.

16. W. Carter Johnson et al., "Prairie Wetland Complexes as Landscape Functional Units in a Changing Climate," *BioScience*, vol. 60, no. 2, pp. 128–38.

17. Johnson, p. 138.

18. Raissa Marks, "Amphibians and Reptiles," *Fish and Wildlife Habitat Management Leaflet*, no. 35, February 2006, p. 4.

19. Hans W. Paerl and Jef Huisman, "Blooms Like It Hot," *Science*, vol. 320, April 4, 2008, p. 57.

20. US Environmental Protection Agency, "Natural Processes in the Great Lakes," July 24, 2008. www.epa.gov.

21. George Kling and Donald Wuebbles, "Executive Summary," *Confronting Climate Change in the Great Lakes Region: Impacts on Our Communities and Ecosystems: A Report of the Union of Concerned Scientists and the Ecological Society of America*, November 2005. www.esa.org.

CHAPTER 4

Plant and Wildlife Health

Plant and wildlife health is a serious concern for conservationists, scientists, businesses, and the general public alike. Global warming, with its potential for violent weather, shifting rainfall patterns, and increased temperatures, is a significant part of a complex web of factors that will affect the health of both plants and wildlife.

Infectious Diseases Are Expanding

Infectious diseases, in particular, pose a serious danger to plants and wildlife on land and in water, and in a time of rapid global warming, many diseases appear to be expanding in range and severity. C. Drew Harvell, professor of ecology and evolutionary biology at Cornell University, and his colleagues assert, "infectious diseases are strong biotic forces that can threaten biodiversity by catalyzing population declines and accelerating extinctions."[1] Biodiversity, the variety of life in a habitat, is essential for the health of all the flora and fauna in any given ecosystem. A sufficiently lethal infectious disease can quickly kill off large numbers of a species, thus causing a steep decrease in the species' population. When enough individuals are killed off, the remaining population suffers a shrunken gene pool, which leads to inbreeding and dangerous mutations. Ultimately, the species may no longer be a viable life form and could eventually become extinct.

Temperature, rainfall, and humidity affect the growth and development of many pathogens (bacteria, viruses, or any microorganism that causes disease). Because global warming will increase temperatures around the world, causing excessive rain in some locations and drought conditions in others, global warming is also changing the way that pathogens interact with the flora and fauna of many ecosystems. As University of Barcelona ecologist Miriam Cotillas and her colleagues report, "Climate change is one of the major challenges for ecosystem conservation."[2]

Global warming is changing the way that pathogens interact with the flora and fauna of many ecosystems.

Specifically, global warming affects both the spread and incidence of disease among plants and animals in three important ways. According to Harvell et al., "Climate warming can increase pathogen development and survival rates, disease transmission, and host susceptibility."[3] Harvell's findings suggest that pathogens may develop more quickly, become more common, and grow hardier. In a warming world, pathogens may be able to spread among a population with greater ease, and the plant or animal infected with the pathogen may be more susceptible to the infection because of other conditions wrought by global warming and human activity.

Plant and Forest Health in a Warming World

Studies show that plant disease epidemics will increase in severity and will move toward higher latitudes with global warming. In other words, the microorganisms and pests that damage trees can expand their range as the world warms, with tropical and subtropical pathogens and pests finding it increasingly possible to survive in areas that previously were too cold for them. North Carolina State University ecologist Robert R. Dunn and his colleagues report that "at temperate and subtropical latitudes, where temperature declines steeply with elevation, and more slowly, but steadily with increasing latitude, insects, vertebrates, and plants have shifted polewards . . . and higher up mountain slopes."[4] Thus, at the same time that plants, vertebrates, and insects are expanding their range, so too are pathogenic bacteria, fungi, viruses, molds, and pests expanding theirs.

In addition, warmer winter temperatures mean that many pathogens will be able to survive the season, leading to greater rates of infection. Likewise, warmer temperatures and an increase in humidity encourage the growth of molds and fungi that can harm plants. In sum, the opportunity for pathogens to infect plants during a period of climate change increases dramatically.

Tree Decline and Mortality

In the Mediterranean Basin of Europe, for example, oak trees are suffering a serious decline brought about by a complex of factors, among them factors associated with climate change. Changes in temperature and rainfall will contribute to a drier and hotter climate for this area, according to Cotillas et al. This shift, in turn, is predicted to place oak trees in the Mediterranean Basin under stress. Furthermore, one of the most serious contributors to oak decline is a root disease caused by the *Phytophthora cinnamomi* fungus. A study by C.M. Brasier of the Forest Research Station in Surrey, England, and J.K. Scott of the Australian Commonwealth Scientific and Industrial Research Organisation concludes that "under conditions of global warming the survival and degree of root disease caused by this fungus seems likely to be enhanced, while the host range of the organism might also be increased."[5] Thus, global warming not only increases the climatic conditions that place trees under stress, it also encourages the growth, survival, and range of pathogenic organisms such as this fungus.

Trees in the United States are also suffering from diseases and pests exacerbated by conditions associated with global warming.

A 2009 study by researchers from the US Geological Survey and the University of Colorado reveals that "tree deaths in the West's old-growth forests have more than doubled in recent decades, likely from regional warming and related drought conditions." Pine, fir, and hemlock trees of all sizes and at a variety of elevations demonstrated serious loss when surveys from 1955–1994 were compared with surveys completed in 1998–2007. The tree deaths are troubling. The researchers note that in addition to contributing to a loss of habitat for wildlife, the tree deaths "also could lead to possible increases in atmospheric carbon dioxide levels contributing to warming, which could stem from lower CO_2 uptake and storage by smaller trees and increased CO_2 emissions from more dead trees on the forest floors."[6]

The study also reveals that most of the recorded tree deaths took place *before* an attack by mountain pine bark beetles, an insect pest that is rapidly killing off huge stands of trees throughout the West. University of Colorado researcher Thomas Vleben states, "Forest entomologists and ecologists agree that warming temperatures are highly favorable to population growth and survival of these beetles. . . . Moisture-stress induced by both warming and reduced snowpack increases tree susceptibility to bark beetle attack."[7]

Forests are also under attack in other parts of the United States. Hemlock trees in the Northeast are succumbing to hemlock wooly adelgids, an exotic insect pest from East Asia. According to horticulturalist Rolf Schilling, "Their rampage on hemlock forests in the Southeast is well documented. Their damage to hemlocks in the Northeast has been limited by one factor: cold winters."[8] Schilling reports, however, that in January 2007, adelgids were active and feeding when they should have been dormant and that, consequently, the pests would be more aggressive and widespread in the spring. This case illustrates how an insect pest can expand its range, increase its numbers, and present a greater threat due to milder temperatures stemming from global warming.

Drought, Flood, and Air Pollution

Warmer weather is not the only factor affecting the health of plants and forests. Indeed, indirect features of global warming create complex and interacting circumstances that work together to present the greatest threat to both flora and fauna. In addition, other factors such as human-induced pollution of water, air, and land interact and amplify the effects of global warming

In the coming decades, it is likely that the earth's average temperature will continue to increase, and that accompanying the higher temperatures will be changes in the incidence and amount of rainfall. Some regions of the world will receive far more rain, and in heavier downpours, than in the past. Other areas will have far less rainfall and an increasing number of extended droughts. Also, scientists predict that there will be more intense, severe storms. These weather events, directly or indirectly linked to global warming, combine with air pollution and toxic runoff to push plants and forests into stress. As environmentalist Su Young Woo from the University of Seoul argues, "Forest decline in several regions of the world is an obvious phenomenon. Probably, air pollution and global warming are . . . the key factors for forest decline due to their greatest negative impact toward forest tree, stand and ecosystem."[9]

When forests are stressed by drought, storm, or pollution, they become more vulnerable to disease and pests. For example, pines in the southeastern United States stressed by drought or by storm damage become susceptible to attack by southern pine beetles, an extraordinarily destructive pest, according to the National Wildlife Federation.

Trees and plants stressed by the conditions of global warming and disease are also vulnerable to yet another attack. Invasive species exploit the weakened condition of diseased, damaged, or drought-stricken plants and trees. These species crowd out the indigenous plant and tree populations and overrun the habitat. The more successful the invasive species proves in a given habitat, the less likely the indigenous species are to survive. Such invasions reduce biodiversity and affect the overall health of the forest. In addition, wildlife that depends on indigenous flora as an integral feature of its habitat can also find itself pushed out of its home.

Wildlife Health and Global Warming

Just as rising temperatures and changes in rainfall are likely to cause an increase in plant pathogens, these conditions are also likely to cause an increase in the abundance of pathogens affecting wildlife. "Environmental change can impinge directly on wildlife heath and survival and, consequently, affect the viability of their populations in various intricate ways," argue London-based zoologists Karina Acevedo-Whitehouse and Amanda L.J. Duffus.[10]

Many of these diseases are vector-borne; that is, the disease-causing microorganism is carried from one animal to the next by a vector, usually some sort of insect or arthropod such as a mosquito, tick, or midge. As the vectors expand under the favorable conditions created by global warming, so, too, do the diseases they carry.

African horse sickness is one such disease. Although the animals most seriously affected are horses and mules, zebras can also be infected. Although zebras do not suffer the most virulent form of the disease, they nonetheless spread the disease to areas previously unaffected by African horse sickness, according to the Center for Food Security and Public Health at Iowa State University. The disease has spread to other continents as well, and as climatic conditions increase vector range and numbers, the disease may become more widespread.

Likewise, mosquitoes bearing avian malaria in Hawaii are extending their range to higher altitudes as the climate warms. This spread may spell disaster for the iiwi honeycreeper, a native bird that is extremely susceptible to avian malaria. According to a study by Carter Atkinson of the US Geological Survey and reported in *Science News* May 27, 2009, a single bite by an infected mosquito will kill the bitten bird 90 percent of the time. Until recently, the cooler, higher elevations have offered the birds a refuge from avian malaria, because the mosquito-vectors cannot tolerate the cooler temperatures. The projected increase in temperature, however, will destroy mosquito-free zones and could lead to extinction for these birds.

Synergistic Effects of Global Warming on Wildlife

Although rising temperatures will affect the health of wildlife, other concurrent features of global warming will also play a role. Drought conditions, for example, are hard on animals and make them more vulnerable to disease. Acevedo-Whitehouse and Duffus note, "Threatened or vulnerable large mammal populations that inhabit . . . critical ecosystems are likely to be severely affected by these climatic changes."[11] The researchers cite as an example the case of a protracted drought in Tanzania leading to an unusually high number of elephant deaths. Longer and more extreme droughts are clearly linked to global warming; thus it is likely that an increasing number of wildlife populations will endure stress, disease, and death.

Furthermore, as noted above, invasive plant species are able to make inroads into a habitat when native plants and trees are under stress from storm damage, drought, or disease. As these plants become the dominant feature of a habitat, animals that depend on native plants for sustenance often suffer from malnutrition. Wildlife stressed by malnutrition is also more vulnerable to disease.

In addition, as indigenous wildlife endures stress, disease, and die-off, alien invasive animal species can overrun a habitat, leading to less biodiversity and contributing to a degraded habitat.

Amphibians in Danger

Scientists around the world are deeply worried about steep declines in amphibian populations. They consider amphibians to

THE RANGE AND DISTRIBUTION OF WILDLIFE DISEASES ARE EXPANDING

Known species diversity before 1995

- P. andersoni
- P. odocoilei

Known species diversity since 1995

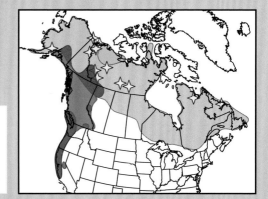

- P. andersoni
- P. odocoilei
- U. pallikuukensis
- ✧ Protostongylidae n. sp

In the Northern Hemisphere, global warming has likely played a role in a northern geographic shift of diseases and parasites. For example, the range of the several species of lung parasites infecting caribou, wild thinhorn sheep, mountain goats, woodland caribou, and black-tailed and mule deer has expanded northward as illustrated above.

Source: "Climate Change and Wildlife Health: Direct and Indirect Effects," *Fact Sheet 2010–3017*, US Geological Survey, March 2010. www.nwhc.usgs.gov/publications/fact_sheets/pdfs/Climate_Change_and_Wildlife_Health.pdf.

be ecological indicators; that is, the health of amphibians is often a reflection of the health of the ecosystem in which they live. Many amphibian species are rapidly facing endangerment or extinction, a cause for serious concern among biologists, ecologists, and environmentalists. According to University of South Florida biologist Jason R. Rohr and his fellow researchers, "More than 32% of amphibian species are threatened, and more than 43% are experiencing some form of population decline." Rohr continues that the planet is "in the midst of a sixth mass extinction event and at the forefront are the amphibians."[12]

In biological classification, class Amphibia includes three orders: Anura (frogs, and toads); Urodela (salamanders and newts) and Gymnophiona (caecilians, which are legless, wormlike creatures). They are cold-blooded vertebrates, meaning that the ambient temperature of their habitat controls their body temperatures. Thus, in cold weather, amphibian body temperatures drop, whereas in hot weather, amphibian body temperatures rise. Amphibians must therefore live within an acceptable range of temperatures. If the weather gets too hot or too cold, amphibians are unable to survive because their body temperatures will become either too hot or too cold. Because global warming causes temperature extremes, it makes amphibian survival more difficult.

Furthermore, amphibians live both in water and on land. They require water, not only for drinking but also for reproduction and health. Amphibians breed in water, and their offspring are water breathing for the first portion of their lives. For example, frogs lay their eggs in water, then the eggs develop into tadpoles that must live in water until they grow legs and lungs and are able to breathe air. In drought conditions, small ponds, rivers, and lakes often dry up, killing off eggs and tadpoles, thus interrupting the amphibian life cycle.

In addition, amphibians require moisture for their skin, through which they absorb water and oxygen. This need makes them particularly vulnerable to dehydration. In times of drought

Amphibians such as the Panama golden frog are vulnerable to the chytrid fungus, although the link between the fungus and climate change is contested. AP Images/Karen Warren.

and high temperatures their skin can dry out, which leads to death for amphibians.

Amphibians are also being attacked in unprecedented numbers by what Rohr et al. call "the most deadly invasive species on the planet (excluding humans), the pathogenic chytrid fungus, *Batrachochytrium dendrobatidis*."[13] Commonly referred to as Bd, the fungus causes the lethal disease chytridiomycosis. The Vredenburg Amphibian Research Group, headed by biologist Vance Vredenburg of San Francisco State University, reports that "Chytridiomycosis is devastating amphibians on a scale never seen before. With over 500 species affected *chytridiomycosis is the worst case in recorded history of a disease driving vertebrate species to extinction*."[14]

Chytridiomycosis and Climate Change

The connection between Bd and global warming, however, is hotly contested. There are individuals who believe that the epidemic is squarely the fault of climate change. As *Science Nation* quotes Vredenburg in 2009, "Some people think it's climate change itself

The Mystery of Costa Rica's Golden Toads

In 1960, researchers in the Reserva Biológica Monteverde discovered a new toad species, the golden toad. Small, with a body length of about 2 inches (5 cm), male golden toads are a shiny, bright orange; the females are dark olive to black, with scarlet, yellow-circled patches. The only known habitat of the toad is the Costa Rican reserve where it was first discovered.

In 1987, there were more than fifteen-hundred golden toads. Yet when researchers returned in 1988, only eight males and two females were seen. In 1989, only one male was seen, and since that time no one has seen another golden toad. The species is now considered to be extinct.

What happened to the golden toad? Many biologists believe that

that's triggering the release of this pathogen from potentially being something that doesn't cause a problem to something that's suddenly really, really deadly . . . It's almost as if humans began dying by the millions from the common cold."[15]

In contrast, researchers such as Southern Illinois zoologist Karen Lips and her research team contend that there is "no evidence to support the hypothesis that climate change has been driving outbreaks of amphibian chytridiomycosis, as has been posited in the climate-linked epidemic hypothesis."[16] Lips's contention that climate change is not the *direct* cause of the chytridiomycosis epidemic does, however, leave room for climate change as an *indirect* factor in the rapid spread of the disease. Furthermore, Lips's research team does not rule out climate change as a direct cause of the epidemic. The researchers contend only that current data does not support such a claim.

It is likely that amphibian extinctions and decline can be linked to a variety of causes, with each one exacerbating the oth-

climate change is the culprit. In the late 1980s, the Costa Rican mountains experienced warmer than usual temperatures and higher than normal aridity. Significantly, these years also experienced a strong El Niño, a temporary change in the climate of the Pacific Ocean that leads to warmer water. Some climate scientists link El Niño to global warming; others see it as part of a natural process of warming and later cooling in the ocean.

Other biologists believe that a fungal disease of amphibians, chytridiomycosis, may have killed off the entire species of golden toads. Still others believe air pollution may have been a factor.

The case of the golden toads illustrates how difficult it is to prove that one factor or another caused a species' extinction. In all likelihood, the toads were stressed by the higher temperatures and aridity, and this stress rendered them vulnerable to attack by disease. Whether the higher temperatures and aridity experienced in the late 1980s were a temporary aberration in so-called normal weather patterns or part of a larger, permanent global climate change remains to be seen.

ers. Climate change, habitat degradation and destruction, new pathogens, and toxic pollution work synergistically to affect the health of amphibians. As Lips et al. argue,

> Disease dynamics are the result of a complex process involving multiple factors related to the hosts, the pathogen, and the environment. . . . Global climate change will directly influence amphibians but will also affect them indirectly through synergisms with habitat alternation, environmental contamination, diseases and other challenges.[17]

Marine Plants and Wildlife

Just as on land, rising temperatures are associated with an increase in the number, range, and longevity of pathogens found in water. Marine bacteria and fungi grow more quickly in warmer waters. In addition, increased water temperatures mean that pathogens can move farther north and south from the equator, expanding their range. Oyster disease, for example, is moving northward along the Atlantic seaboard, affecting oysters in the Chesapeake Bay area.

In addition, warmer waters can be dangerous to marine creatures for two important reasons. First, as ecologists Kevin D. Lafferty, James W. Porter, and Susan E. Ford note, "Higher temperatures may stress organisms, increasing their susceptibility to disease. . . . Tropical marine organisms are naturally much closer to their upper lethal temperature than to their lower lethal temperature and this may put them at a disadvantage in fighting disease if temperature increases." That is, marine organisms that live in the tropics are able to survive somewhat lower temperatures better than higher temperatures. Lafferty and his colleagues further assert that as ocean temperatures rise, the available oxygen in the water decreases, causing a change in marine life metabolism. This characteristic of warming is "universally stressful for marine invertebrates and fishes."[18]

The health of marine mammals is also likely to suffer, particularly in the Arctic. Polar bears and seals are more prone to disease in warmer temperatures. Moreover, as biologists Amy Greer, Victoria Ng, and David Fisman argue, "Changing ecosystems . . . disrupt the ecology of wildlife populations in ways that are likely to increase the risk of zoonotic disease."[19] Zoonotic diseases are animal diseases that can be passed to humans.

Coral: A Case Study in Disease and Global Warming

Coral reefs offer a clear example of the complex ways global warming affects the health of marine flora and fauna. Tiny animals known as polyps create coral. As polyps grow, they secrete limestone around them that serves as a skeleton. Colonies of coral build large reefs in shallow ocean waters. Lafferty et al. rightly note that the health of corals is of great importance, as the creatures "create habitat for whole communities."[20] Coral reefs also protect shorelines from damaging waves and storm surges. Coral reefs have been seriously damaged around the world in recent decades, however. Biologists Laura D. Mydlarz and Elizabeth S. McGinty, and ecologist C. Drew Harvell attribute the increase in coral mortality to global warming: "The effects of temperature stress are apparent in the two main physiological conditions that currently affect corals on a global scale: bleaching and disease."[21]

Interestingly, coral lives in a symbiotic relationship with an alga called zooxanthellae. Symbiosis is a relationship in which each partner contributes a condition necessary to the survival of the other. According to *New York Times* science journalist Cornelia Dean, "Coral polyps shelter the algae and as the tiny plants photosynthesize they produce sugars the corals rely on for food."[22] Coral bleaching occurs when the algae die off; without the algae's brown or green pigmentation, the coral takes on a "bleached" look of pure white. Because the algae provide food for the corals, their deaths presage coral death as well. Lafferty and his colleagues stress that "the vast majority of bleaching is caused by elevated water temperature."[23]

Diseases such as aspergillosis, white pox, and black band flourish under higher temperatures and are able to attack the vulnerable coral that suffer from malnutrition as a result of algal die-off. Indeed, most scientists believe that "infectious diseases are thought to be key to this mass coral mortality, and many reef ecologists suspect that anomalously high ocean temperatures contribute to the increased incidence and severity of disease outbreaks," according to marine scientist John F. Bruno and his research partners.[24] The synergistic effect of algal die-off and opportunistic infectious diseases puts coral reefs seriously at risk as a result of warmer ocean temperatures. Mydlarz and her colleagues concur, linking coral bleaching and an increase in infectious diseases to warmer sea-surface temperatures. She predicts that "coral mortality due to climate-associated stress is likely to increase as the oceans get warmer and more acidic."[25]

Although there is some evidence that some symbiotic algae can withstand higher ocean temperatures, these algae do not occur naturally everywhere, according to Dean. Some scientists have suggested introducing the heat-resistant algae into coral reef systems that are experiencing bleaching. Such a plan, however, seems fraught with danger, as the outcome of such an introduction is completely unknown at this time, and could create a bigger problem than it solves.

Notes

1. C. Drew Harvell et al, "Climate Warming and Disease Risks for Terrestrial and Marine Biota," *Science*, vol. 296, no. 5576, June 21, 2002, p. 2158.
2. Miriam Cotillas et al., "Growth Response of Mixed Mediterranean Oak Coppices to Rainfall Reduction: Could Selective Thinning Have Any Influence on It?" *Forest Ecology and Management*, vol. 258, no. 7, September 15, 2009, p. 1677.
3. Harvell, "Climate Warming and Disease Risks for Terrestrial and Marine Biota," p. 2158.
4. Robert R. Dunn et al., "The Sixth Mass Extinction: Are Most Endangered Species Parasites and Mutualists?" *Proceedings of the Royal Society*, vol. 276, May 27, 2009, p. 3041.
5. C.M. Brasier and J.K. Scott, "European Oak Declines and Global Warming: A Theoretical Assessment with Special Reference to the Activity of *Phytophthora cinnamomi*," *Eppo Bulletin*, vol., 24, no. 1, p. 221.
6. University of Colorado News Center, "New Study Links Western Tree Mortality to Warming Temperatures, Water Stress," January 22, 2009. www.colorado.edu.
7. Quoted in University of Colorado News Center, "New Study Links Western Tree Mortality to Warming Temperatures, Water Stress."
8. Rolf Schilling, "Global Warming Adelgid Alert," New England Wildflower Society, 2007. www.newfs.org.
9. SuYoung Woo, "Forest Decline of the World: A Linkage with Air Pollution and Global Warming," *African Journal of Biotechnology*, vol. 8, no. 25, December 29, 2009, p. 7413.
10. Karina Acevedo-Whitehouse and Amanda L.J. Duffus, "Effects of Environmental Change on Wildlife Health," *Philosophical Transactions of the Royal Society: Biological Sciences*, vol. 364, November 27, 2009, pp. 3431–32.
11. Acevedo-Whitehouse, "Effects of Environmental Change on Wildlife Health," p. 3433.
12. Jason R. Rohr et al., "Evaluating the Links Between Climate, Disease Spread, and Amphibian Declines," *PNAS*, vol.105, no. 45, November 11, 2008, p. 17436.
13. Rohr, "Evaluating the Links Between Climate, Disease Spread, and Amphibian Declines," p. 17436.
14. Vredenburg Amphibian Research Group, "Chytridiomycosis," Vredenburg Lab: Amphibian Biodiversity and Conservation, 2010. web.me.com/vancevredenburg/Vances_site/Research.html.
15. Quoted in *Science Nation*, "Disappearing Frogs: Trying to Save the World's Amphibians," November 2, 2009. www.nsf.gov.
16. Karen R. Lips et al., "Riding the Wave: Reconciling the Roles of Disease and Climate Change in Amphibian Declines," *PLos*, March 25, 2008. www.plosbiology.org.
17. Lips, "Riding the Wave."

18. Kevin D. Lafferty, James W. Porter, and Susan E. Ford, "Are Diseases Increasing in the Ocean?" *Annual Review of Ecology, Evolution, and Systematics*, vol. 35, 2004, pp. 30–40. www.jstor.org.
19. Amy Greer, Victoria Ng, and David Fisman, "Climate Change and Infectious Disease in North America: The Road Ahead," *CMAJ*, 178, no. 6, March 11, 2008, p. 720.
20. Lafferty, "Are Diseases Increasing in the Ocean?"p. 47.
21. Laura D. Mydlarz, Elizabeth S. McGinty, and C. Drew Harvell, "What Are the Physiological and Immunological Responses of Coral to Climate Warming and Disease?" *The Journal of Experimental Biology*, vol. 213, 2010, p. 934.
22. Cornelia Dean, "Corals Partner Up with Heat-Resistant Algae," *New York Times Dot Earth*, February 18, 2010. dotearth.blogs.nytimes.com.
23. Lafferty, "Are Diseases Increasing in the Ocean?" p. 40.
24. John F. Bruno et al., "Thermal Stress and Coral Cover as Drivers of Coral Disease Outbreaks," *PLoS Biology*, vol. 5, no. 6, June 2007, p. 1227.
25. Mydlarz, "What Are the Physiological and Immunological Responses of Coral to Climate Warming and Disease?" p. 934.

CHAPTER 5

Animal Immune and Reproductive Systems

The survival of a species depends most importantly on two factors, factors that find expression in individual members of the species but also have far-reaching implications for the species as a whole. First, an animal must have the ability to ward off infectious diseases in order not to succumb to a wide array of bacterial, viral, and fungal infections. Second, an animal must be able to reproduce. Although the individual animal will certainly die from natural or human-induced causes, if the animal has been able to pass on its genetic code to the next generation, the species will continue. When the reproductive health or the reproductive rate of a species is compromised, however, the population decreases. If the population decrease is steep or prolonged, it could signal a slide into extinction for the species.

Animal Immune Systems and Weather-Related Events

The effects of climate change may seriously compromise animal immune systems through a variety of means, some the direct result of rising temperatures, others the indirect results of a warming planet. Higher temperatures may stress both plants and wildlife. Each species has an optimal temperature range in which its metabolism operates most efficiently. Although species may be able to survive temporary fluctuations in temperature, easily overcoming the occasional chilly evening or blistering hot afternoon, when the average temperatures of a habitat rise or fall, and the number of days exhibiting extreme temperatures rises, both wildlife and plants suffer stress. That is, their metabolisms have to work harder and less efficiently in order for them to survive. When an organism is chronically stressed, the overall effect is to weaken its immune system, thus rendering the organism vulnerable to life-threatening infections.

Another way that climate change is likely to compromise animal immune systems is through changing rainfall patterns. Global warming models suggest that larger areas of the earth will experience more severe and more prolonged drought conditions as the climate changes. Drought can damage animal immune systems both directly and indirectly. First, a lack of fluid intake, directly caused by a reduction in available water that is characteristic of drought conditions, stresses any organism. The long-term effects of stress are damaged immune systems. Second, drought invariably leads to the death of plant life and vegetation. When a habitat experiences drought, there is less available food for animal species in the habitat. Animals initially will choose alternate food sources that might not be optimal for their nutritional needs but that can, nevertheless, sustain life. When even these food sources begin to disappear, the animal will begin to suffer malnutrition long before it is in risk of starving to death. Malnutrition itself is a dangerous condition, however, as it damages the immune system, again leaving the animal vulnerable to bacterial, viral, or fungal infections.

Climate change models also demonstrate that rainfall may increase in some areas, however, and that the number of heavy rain events and damaging storms will increase. These conditions may lead to flooding, another factor that can compromise animal immune systems. Floods may destroy food sources, leading to malnutrition and starvation that stress animals and compromise their immune systems. Perhaps even more insidious is the damage flooding does to animals when it occurs in industrial or urban areas. Urban and industrial settings are repositories of chemicals, heavy metals, and other toxins. When floodwaters sweep through such an area, they often carry these toxins into animal habitats, thus exposing the animal to poisons. Those animals that survive the initial onslaught of floodwaters often experience damaged or faulty immune systems later as a result. In addition, because floodwaters also carry dangerous pathogens, animals with under-functioning immune systems may fall ill from bacterial infections.

An Increased Risk of Infectious Disease

In addition, climate change may lead to the expansion of disease-causing pathogens into areas where indigenous species have little or no immune response to the new illnesses. Ecologist C. Drew Harvell and his colleagues affirm that "links between climate change and diseases will increase the severity of threats associated with climate warming. . . . Epidemics caused when [emergent pathogens] infect new hosts with little resistance or tolerance may lead to population declines."[1]

Similarly, in a review of relevant literature, zoologist Karina Acevedo-Whitehouse and zoologist Amanda L.J. Duffus affirm the impact of stress on animal immune and reproductive systems. They write, "Animals faced with nutritional or hydric stress will 'take the risk' of investing less in reproduction or in maintaining optimal immune responses because in that situation it is more important to reduce immediate risk of death from starvation, malnutrition or dehydration." They conclude that animal populations struggling with improper nutrition or an inadequate food supply brought on by drought "will be at a higher risk of acquiring endemic or novel infections."[2]

The Effects of Habitat Loss and Fragmentation on Immunity

As discussed in Chapter 2 and Chapter 3, habitat loss and fragmentation are serious problems for many organisms. In addition to the direct effects of habitat loss and fragmentation on animal health and well-being, however, there are other indirect effects. A reduction in habitat can put organisms into closer contact with predators, leading not only to death as a result of predation, but also to increased stress as animals attempt to escape predators and protect their young. Chronic stress, as noted above, compromises the immune system.

Furthermore, habitat reduction can lead to a reduction in food sources, again placing the animal in stress through malnutrition. Fragmented and reduced habitats can also limit the gene pool available to a species, thus leading to inbreeding. Inbreeding magnifies any problems with the immune system and produces weakened offspring. As Acevedo-Whitehouse and Duffus note, "Low levels of genetic diversity tend to be correlated with reduced fitness and lowered evolutionary potential."[3]

Climate Change and Animal Reproduction

Climate change also seriously affects species viability through its impact on reproductive cycles. Stress, caused by malnutrition, diseases, or toxins, not only damages animals' immune systems, it can also affect whether an animal reproduces. In time of famine, flood, or disease, animals may fail to mate. Even if the animal successfully mates, however, the mating may not result in conception. Thus, reproduction may happen less often, or not at all.

Climate change can also lead to the loss of important breeding grounds for a variety of species. The Prairie Pothole region of North America, for example, is one of the most important sites of temporary wetlands for migrating birds, as it provides their primary breeding habitat. According to a large-scale study by the US Department of the Interior, the area is "the most productive habitat for breeding ducks in the world. It produces 50–80% of the continent's ducks, even though it represents only 10% of the continent's total wetland area." The study cites climate change models that predict a reduction of ponds in the Prairie Pothole region by up to two thirds. This reduction in wetlands will affect migrating waterfowl and lead to population declines. As the study concludes, "If pond numbers decline by [two thirds], duck numbers in [the] north-central United States are expected to be reduced. Losing even a fraction of these habitats would impact continental duck populations."[4]

Changing Seasons and Reproduction

One of the most devastating effects global warming has on animal reproduction is changing seasonality. That is, global warming is causing the seasons to shift. In many parts of the world, spring is arriving earlier than normal and summers are lasting longer.

For example, environmental writer David Adam, writing in the British newspaper *The Guardian*, reports that "global warming could be disrupting the delicate balance of nature." He summarizes an exhaustive study demonstrating the foreshortening of winter and the effects of earlier springs and summers on wildlife. On average, according to Adam, "the study showed the seasonal timing of reproduction and population growth shifted forward by eleven days [between 1976 and 2005] and that the change has accelerated recently."[5] The study's lead author, biologist Stephen Thackery, summarizes the problem with such shifts in seasons: "This is about the asynchronisation of events during the year. Animals and birds time their reproduction to coincide with periods when there will be an abundance of food. If changes mean there is not enough food available then this could have negative consequences for their offspring."[6]

The impact of seasonality on animal reproduction cannot be overestimated. As Thackery implies, most animals have developed a complicated system of timing for mating, birthing, and rearing of young that depend upon temperature, available water, abundant food, and other factors. Climate change is affecting this timing. In the words of the Audubon Society, "Egg-laying, flowering, and spawning are occurring earlier for many species, in some cases disrupting delicate cycles that ensure that insects and other food are available for young animals."[7]

HOW THE CHANGING ENVIRONMENT AFFECTS ANIMAL IMMUNITY AND REPRODUCTION

Potential effects of anthropogenic environmental change on wildlife health.

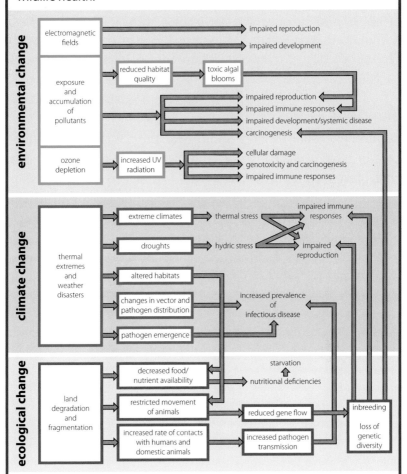

This illustration intends to depict the intricate and multiple ways by which changes to the environment can affect health. Regardless of the level at which the changes occur (environmental, climactic, and ecological), these will in turn alter other physical and biological processes, eventually increasing the risk of starvation and exposure to diseases. At an individual level, environmental changes will affect health by weakening immune responses, impairing development, and causing systemic disease or cancer.

Source: Karina Acevedo-Whitehouse and Amanda J.L. Duffus, "Effects of Environmental Change on Wildlife Health, Figure 2," *Philosophical Transactions of the Royal Society: Biological Sciences*, vol. 364, November 27, 2009, p. 3433. Reproduced by permission of the publisher and authors.

Nowhere has the change in the timing of seasons been more pronounced than in the far North. The Danish environmentalist Toke T. Høye of the Department of Arctic Environment, University of Aarhus, and his research partners have documented "extremely rapid climate-induced advancement of flowering, emergence and egg-laying in a wide array of species in a high-arctic ecosystem." Moreover, the team's research reveals, "In the Arctic . . . temperatures are increasing at nearly double the global average."[8]

The Case of the Lemmings

Lemmings, small rodents found near the Arctic Circle, offer a case in point concerning the complicated role that shifting seasons present in reproductive cycles. Writer Patrick Tucker summarizes, "A longer summer would seem to be good for the lemmings as this would increase the time available for the younger

A shortening of the winter season has a detrimental effect on lemmings, which breed during the winter. Hans Dekkers/Foto Natura/Minden Pictures/Getty Images.

members of the species to forage and grow before the onset of harsher conditions." As Tucker notes, however, lemmings breed in the winter. Early-onset spring and latecoming summer indicate a shortening of the winter season. Thus, there would be less time available for lemmings to breed. And it is not only lemmings affected in this scenario: Tucker points out, "The change in lemming breeding habits will likely alter [their] predators' habitats as well. . . . All of these disruptions will add to pressure that the animals already face from encroaching populations of other alien species attracted to the north's rapidly rising temperatures."[9]

The Complications of Adaptation

Some species will adapt to the changes in seasonality by adjusting their reproductive cycles and timing, or by moving their habitats toward higher latitudes. Even in instances of warmer temperatures that would appear to be beneficial to a species, the increase in temperature comes at a cost. Biologist Nicholas Rodenhouse and his fellow researchers reviewed relevant literature on the effects of climate change on the animals of the northeastern forests of the United States. They note, "Increasing temperatures will likely be accompanied by earlier calling dates [the dates frogs and other amphibians begin to vocalize] and oviposition [egg-laying] for pond breeding amphibians." They hypothesize that those species that are able to move to earlier breeding might enjoy an advantage over later breeders because their offspring would be larger and better able to compete for food.

Rodenhouse et al. also write, "Under warmer conditions . . . tadpole survival would also be affected by the earlier drying of ponds."[10] This shift, in turn, could lead to more tadpoles competing for less food in smaller ponds. In addition, tadpoles could risk drying out and dying if the ponds in which they were born dry out before the tadpoles have fully developed. Thus, even though warmer temperatures and shifting seasons appear at first to be a positive change for some species, on closer inspection it is clear that situation is not quite so simple. Changing one part of a species' reproductive cycle will surely have ramifications for the entire cycle, and it is unlikely that all will be uniformly positive.

Although it is possible that the caribou might be able to adjust their reproductive cycles, given enough time, the rapid rate of warming in the far north is unlikely to offer a sufficient period for adaptation.

Likewise, according to a publication of the Union of Concerned Scientists and the Ecological Society of America prepared by ecologist George W. King and others, many species of the Great Lakes will suffer the mixed blessings of climate change. Although some fishes would grow faster in warmer weather, they would also have to consume more food to sustain their size. Food may or may not be in adequate supply. King also reports that, in the Great Lakes region, "Changes in the timing and severity of flood pulses are likely to reduce safe breeding sites, especially for amphibians, migratory shorebirds and waterfowl."[11]

Some Species Cannot Adapt

Other species may be unable to adapt, resulting in declines in their populations. Pennsylvania State University biology professor Eric Post, for example, offers migratory caribou in Low Arctic Greenland and elsewhere as a species that is not adjusting well to climate change. Post reveals these populations are declining because "the caribou have not been able to adjust their calving season to keep it synchronized with changes in plant growth." In the past, caribou have timed their calving to coincide with abundant food. Now, however, according to Post, "The time when the females need the most food no longer matches the time of maximum food availability, so fewer calves survive."[12] Although it is possible that the caribou might be able to adjust their reproductive cycles, given enough time, the rapid rate of warming in the far north is unlikely to offer a sufficient period for adaptation.

Migrating Birds and Changing Seasons

Migrating birds also provide another stark example of what can happen when animals' internal timing does not match the change in seasonality. The Audubon Society reports, "Spring migration is occurring earlier and fall migration later in many species. For example, 25 migratory bird species are arriving in Manitoba, Canada, earlier than they did 63 years ago; only two are arriving later."[13] Changes in seasonality are particularly devastating for "birds that time their migration by day length rather than by weather," according to King. Because the length of days is not changing, even as temperatures and seasons are, such birds have little hope of adapting to the new reality of global warming. King notes, "Long-distance migratory birds such as scarlet tanagers, warblers, thrushes, and flycatchers depend on trees and caterpillars for food. . . . Food sources may be severely reduced when they arrive in the Great Lakes region."[14] Reduced food sources can lead to malnutrition and starvation for the birds, as well as to a failure to reproduce.

Furthermore, migrating waterfowl depend on temporary wetlands for reproducing and for fledging their young. If spring begins early in their traditional breeding grounds, it means that by the time the birds arrive, the temporary wetlands may no longer be present. In cases where there is no water, the birds simply cannot reproduce. In addition, these temporary wetlands are also in danger of disappearing because of warmer temperatures and less rainfall. The combination could be lethal for migrating birds.

The Road to Extinction

Thus, global warming appears to endanger species' viability through indirectly damaging immune systems and through compromising the phenological (or life-cycle) processes associated with reproduction. Organisms with immune systems that are unable to protect against emerging pathogens are susceptible to illness or death, sometimes in epidemic proportions. It is important to remember that this is an indirect effect of global

The Life Cycle of the Mallard

Mallards are among the best known of all wild ducks in North America, and they are common throughout Europe as well. Mallards, like all migratory waterfowl, depend on the availability of wetlands for their entire life cycle.

Mallards migrate to the southern United States and Central America in the late fall and early winter. They select mates each fall in a process known as "pair bonding." They return north in the spring to breed, usually in late March or early April. The mallard pair attempts to find a safe spot to lay its eggs. This location is usually near the place the female herself was hatched. The mallards search for spots near water that have good cover, such as grasses, weeds, and a variety of other types of vegetation that are typical of marshy wetlands.

The female lays eight to twelve eggs, one per day. She then incubates her eggs for up to twenty-eight days, keeping the eggs warm by brooding—sitting gently atop the eggs. Down, the soft feathers from her underside, cover the eggs, keeping them warm and camouflaged.

Once the ducklings hatch, the mother must immediately take them

warming; higher temperatures, extreme weather events, and habitat loss and fragmentation do not directly affect the immune system. These factors place organisms under stress, however, and long-term, chronic stress compromises an animal's immune system. When the population of a species falls rapidly because of disease, the species can become endangered and ultimately may become extinct.

Global warming is having both direct and indirect effects, however, on the phenology of many species. Reproduction is a complicated cycle, tied to weather, food availability, and the length of days, among many other factors. Climate change affects the ability of a species to reproduce indirectly by placing stress on organisms. When an animal is in danger of starvation because of extreme weather events, or is being harried by an into a nearby water source that will provide food. Ducklings are able to swim and find their own food right after hatching, but they need their mother to provide protection and direction. The baby ducks eat insects, crustaceans, and plants. The ducklings need another two months of development before they are able to fly.

If a mallard's nest is destroyed, or if the pair is sufficiently harassed in its first choice of nesting site, the birds can sometimes renest several times. Fewer eggs will be laid each time, however, as the female's stored energy diminishes with each renesting.

For mallards, successful reproduction depends upon the timing of migration, breeding, brooding, hatching, and fledging their young. If migration begins too late, because of warm and late winters, the entire cycle can be thrown off. If spring arrives too early, mallards may find that the wetlands they depend on for nesting and hatching their young have disappeared. Furthermore, food sources may no longer be abundant if ducklings hatch too late.

Although mallards are not endangered, their life cycle illustrates how vulnerable all migratory waterfowl are to changes in the seasons brought about by global warming.

vasive predator, the animal will choose to survive rather than engage in the reproductive cycle. Climate change directly affects reproduction in many species because it is causing earlier springs, longer summers, and shorter winters. Such change disrupts the natural timing of events that lead to breeding and birthing, and it renders an organism's offspring vulnerable to starvation, dehydration, or predation. When a species is unable to mate, birth, or rear its young, the species' population necessarily declines. In some cases, populations can decline steeply and rapidly, placing the entire species in danger of extinction.

Notes

1. C. Drew Harvell et al., "Climate Warming and Disease Risks for Terrestrial and Marine Biota," *Science*, vol. 296, June 21, 2002, p. 2161.

2. Karina Acevedo-Whitehouse and Amanda L.J. Duffus, "Effects of Environmental Change on Wildlife Health," *Philosophical Transactions of the Royal Society B*, vol. 364, 2009, p. 3433.

3. Acevedo-Whitehouse, "Effects of Environmental Change on Wildlife Health," p. 3431.

4. US Department of the Interior, *The State of the Birds: 2010 Report on Climate Change*, North American Bird Conservation Initiative, 2010, p. 26.

5. David Adam, "Earlier Springs Could Destroy Delicate Balance of UK Wildlife, Study Shows," *The Guardian*, February 9, 2010. www.guardian.co.uk.

6. Quoted in Adam, "Earlier Springs Could Destroy Delicate Balance of UK Wildlife, Study Shows."

7. Audubon Society, "Impacts on Birds and Wildlife," 2010. www.audubon.org.

8. Toke T. Høy et al., "Rapid Advancement of Spring in the High Arctic," *Current Biology*, vol. 17, no. 12, June 19, 2007, p. 449.

9. Patrick Tucker, "Arctic Species at the Cliff's Edge: New Paper Models Changes for Arctic Species Due to Climate Change," *The Futurist*, vol. 44, no. 1, January–February 2010, p. 8.

10. Nicholas L. Rodenhouse, "Climate Change Effects on Native Fauna of Northeastern Forests, *Canadian Journal of Forest Research*, vol. 39, 2009, p. 254.

11. George W. King et al., "Executive Summary," *Confronting Climate Change in the Great Lakes Region: Impacts on Our Communities and Ecosystems*, Union of Concern Scientists and the Ecological Society of America, 2005. www.ucsusa.org.

12. Eric Post, "Dramatic Biological Responses to Global Warming in the Arctic," Pennsylvania State University, September 10, 2009. www.science.psu.edu.

13. Audubon Society, "Impacts on Birds and Wildlife."

14. King, "Executive Summary."

CHAPTER 6

Air and Water Quality

Scientists overwhelmingly believe that global warming is caused by greenhouse gases, and that greenhouse gases in the atmosphere are increasing dramatically because of human activities such as the burning of fossil fuels. In addition, other pollutants contribute to the overall warming of the planet. Not surprisingly, these same factors contribute to a reduction of air quality and water quality all over the globe. The increase in temperatures and weather changes associated with global warming further degrade air and water quality. Thus, both the causes *and* effects of global warming present a serious challenge to the air and water necessary for the survival of nature and wildlife of all sorts.

The Carbon Cycle

It is important to understand first the global carbon cycle as a starting point for a discussion of how global warming affects air and water quality. Carbon is the basis of all life on earth. The global carbon cycle describes how carbon atoms circulate through living organisms, the ocean, the earth's crust, and the atmosphere, a process that can take millions of years. In brief, carbon enters the atmosphere as carbon dioxide (CO_2), the result of the respiration and decay of plants and animals; the release of CO_2 from warm ocean waters; volcanic eruption; the reaction of limestone to acid rain; and the burning of fossil fuels. Carbon is absorbed from the atmosphere by plants as part of the process of photosynthesis, and by cold areas of the ocean. Areas that absorb more carbon than they release are called carbon sinks.

When the carbon cycle is in balance, roughly the same amount of carbon is released as is absorbed. When more carbon is released than can be absorbed, however, the excess CO_2 is trapped in the earth's atmosphere and leads to the warming of the planet.

Indeed, carbon dioxide is the major greenhouse gas raising the earth's temperature. According to Richard Houghton, senior scientist for carbon research at the Woods Hole Research Center, "The concentration of CO_2 in the atmosphere has already increased by 30% since the start of the industrial revolution around the middle of the 19th century and will continue to increase unless societies choose to change their ways."[1] He further asserts that most of the increase stems from growing industrial emissions, although a quarter of the increase can be attributed to the clearing of forests.

In sum, as ocean temperatures rise and as large swaths of forest are either cut down or die from disease, these carbon sinks are unable to function effectively. This impairment allows levels of atmospheric CO_2 to rise and leads to further warming.

Global Warming and Ozone Formation

Air quality in many parts of the world suffers from a host of assaults. It can be difficult to tease out the direct and specific role of global warming among them; it is possible to see global warming as part of a synergistic process, however. That is, global warming, industrialization, agricultural practices, and urbanization, among others, work together to create more damage to the air than any one factor could create alone.

Scientists have noted an increase in the levels of ozone, the most common air pollutant in the lower atmosphere. Ozone (O_3) is a toxic gas composed of three oxygen atoms, whereas the oxygen that humans and animals breathe is composed of two (O_2). According to the US Environmental Protection Agency (EPA),

"At ground-level [ozone] is created by a chemical reaction between oxides of nitrogen (NO_x) and volatile compounds (VOCs) in the presence of sunlight. . . . Motor vehicle exhaust and industrial emissions, gasoline vapors, and chemical solvents as well as natural sources emit NO_x and VOC that help form ozone."[2]

Hot weather and sunlight can increase the amount of ozone at ground level. Large cities, where gasoline emissions are high and large expanses of paved areas result in the urban "heat island" effect, are especially susceptible to such ozone formation. Heat islands occur because urban areas are covered by concrete rather than plant life, and they tend to absorb and hold more heat than, say, a forest. Thus, the larger amounts of NO_x and VOC found in urban areas combined with higher temperatures work together to create sometimes-dangerous levels of ozone concentration in the air. Indeed, ozone is the primary component of smog, a common sight in many large urban areas. Rural areas, are not free from ozone pollution, however. Winds carry ozone and other pollutants far from their sources, sometimes contaminating the air in what might otherwise be pristine rural areas.

Ozone, Global Warming, and Nature

Because heat and sunlight are factors in ozone formation, global warming is projected to increase the amount of ground-level ozone. Not only is global warming raising temperatures around the earth, places will also experience more sunlight, particularly in times of drought. Combined with the increasing levels of NO_x and VOC, the increased heat and sunlight have the potential of creating more ground-level ozone. This possibility is dangerous because ozone has been shown to damage the lungs of both humans and animals when inhaled at high concentrations over extended periods of time.

In addition, ozone damages trees and plants. Stephen Sitch and his colleagues from England's Hadley Centre for Climate Change Research note that plants and soil remove carbon dioxide emissions from the atmosphere, thereby easing global warming.

They argue, however, that "Increased carbon dioxide and ozone levels can both lead to stomatal closure [of leaf pores], which reduces the uptake of either gas." The closure of leaf pores protects the plants from damage from ozone. In addition, however, the closure of leaf pores also reduces the amount of carbon dioxide the plant is able to absorb and remove from the atmosphere. As Stich and his colleagues continue, "We find a significant suppression of the global land-carbon sink as increases in ozone concentrations affect plant productivity."[3] In other words, the interaction of CO_2 and ozone leads to a reduction in the effectiveness of the land-carbon sink, which in turn leads to a build up of CO_2, and the production of even more ozone.

Acid Rain, Nature, and Wildlife

The same factors that contribute to the formation of ground-level ozone also create what is known as "acid rain." Quite simply, acid rain is precipitation that has a higher than normal amount of NO_x and sulfur dioxide (SO_2). According to the EPA, "In the United States, roughly 2/3 of all SO_2 and 1/4 of all NO_x come from electric power generation that relies on burning fossil fuels, like coal."[4] Gasoline-powered automobiles also contribute. Regular rain is slightly acidic, with pH values averaging 5, although some scientists cite a pH of 5.6 to be normal. Rains that carry these pollutants, however, often are measured at pH 4, an acid solution.

To be clear, acid rain has not been caused by global warming, although the same factors that contribute to global warming create acid rain. Nevertheless, there is a clear connection between acid rain and global warming, in that acid rain affects trees, plants, lakes, streams, and wildlife. Any reduction of forests and plant life represents damage to land-based carbon sinks.

Acid Rain and Soil

Acid rain can also seriously reduce the amount of soil calcium in forests. Greg Lawrence of the US Geological Survey notes that soils can often buffer the harm caused by acid rain because of calcium content that neutralizes the acid. There is a limit to how much acid that calcium can buffer before it is completely depleted. When such depletion occurs, aluminum is taken up by plants. Lawrence states, "Aluminum is harmful to everything, from diatoms to spruce trees."[5] Lawrence believes that acid rain's impact is so great that it needs to be included in research on climate change.

Likewise, Syracuse University environmental systems engineer Charles Driscoll also believes that acid rain is a serious problem for forests because of calcium and magnesium depletion. He notes,

> Acid rain has the most severe impact in high elevation forests. These areas are also sensitive to changing climate. . . . Our work suggests that warmer temperatures [increase] the breakdown of soil organic matter, which has accumulated large quantities of nitrogen from acid rain inputs. A warmer climate causes nitric acid to be leached from soil and acidify the soil or water. Our model calculations suggest that this effect may occur over the next 100 years or so.[6]

On other words, the problem of acid in forests, lakes, and streams derives not only from the rain but also from warming temperatures. As calcium and magnesium in the soil become depleted, the soil becomes more acidic, eventually breaking down and releasing the stored nitric acid, leading to even further acidification.

Not all studies bear out the damage caused by nitrogen, however. Jennifer Donovan reports that, according to Andrew Burton and other researchers from Michigan Technological University, "moderate increases in temperature and nitrogen from atmospheric pollution actually improve forest productivity." Burton and his team concluded a twenty-year study in 2008 and found that trees grow faster and store more carbon when exposed to acid rain. Burton further states, "It may well be that increasing temperature and nitrogen deposition are good things, up to a point."[7] Burton also warns, however, that there may be a "tipping point" after which increases in acid rain would harm forests, rather than help them. What all of these studies suggest, however, is that the impact of acid rain on the health of forests and plant life must be considered in any discussion of climate change.

Global Warming and Ocean Oxygen Depletion

In addition to global warming's impact on air quality, water quality is also being affected by climate change. The ocean and all plant and wildlife contained therein face particular risk from oxygen depletion, algal overgrowth, and water acidification.

Growing evidence suggests that some parts of the ocean are becoming depleted of oxygen. Researchers also demonstrated in 2008 that oxygen-depleted areas are expanding as the ocean warms. The study, led by Lothar Stramm from the Leibniz Institute of Marine Sciences and Janet Sprintall, a physical oceanographer at the Scripps Institution of Oceanography, found that oxygen levels of some areas of the tropical ocean are declining and that oxygen-poor, or hypoxic, areas are expanding. "The width of the low-oxygen zone is expanding deeper but also shoaling toward the ocean surface,"[8] asserts Sprintall.

In a 2010 article appearing in *The Olympian* (Olympia, Washington), writer Les Blumenthal also addresses the causes and implications of expanding hypoxic areas. He reports, "As ocean temperatures rise, the warmer water on the surface acts as a cap, which interferes with the natural circulation that normally allows deeper waters that are already oxygen-depleted to reach the surface. It's on the surface where ocean waters are recharged with oxygen from the air." He describes a 1,200-square-mile (3,108-sq.-km) hypoxic area found off the United States' Northwest coast in 2006, close enough "to shore that you could hit it with a baseball."[9] Oregon State University oceanographer

Francis Chan warns, "If the Earth continues to warm, the expectation is we will have lower and lower oxygen levels."[10]

Habitat Loss and Fragmentation from Ocean Oxygen Depletion

Oxygen depletion represents ocean habitat loss and fragmentation. Areas that have become depleted of oxygen are, in effect, dead zones where neither plants nor wildlife can live. But even in areas where oxygen is only partially depleted, plants and wildlife still struggle for survival. Low-oxygen levels stress organisms, forcing their metabolisms to work harder. As a consequence, such organisms are often vulnerable to disease and suffer from poor reproduction.

Oxygen depletion also limits areas where predatory fish and other marine organisms can hunt. This can put pressure on food supplies as the concentration of predatory fish increases in areas that can support them, resulting in inadequate food supplies, further stressing marine organisms.

Moreover, oxygen depletion limits biodiversity in these areas. A potential exists for harmful overgrowth of organisms that can tolerate low-oxygen habitats to the detriment of native species. Jellyfish, for example, are normally kept in check by small fish that eat jellyfish young. Most fish, however, unlike jellyfish, are unable to survive hypoxic areas. According to *Time* science writer Stephan Faris, "When the fish population plummets, the tables are turned. By preying on the eggs and larvae of the few surviving fish, the jellyfish prevent them from replenishing their numbers and quickly take their place."[11] In addition, tropical jellyfish are expanding their range because of warming seas. As a result of these two climate-related changes, jellyfish populations around the world are rapidly rising.

Harmful Algal Blooms

The overgrowth of yet another organism is degrading ocean water quality. With increasing regularity, harmful algal blooms

Case Study: The Invasion of the Jellyfish

Anyone who has spent time at the shore in warm weather has probably had an encounter with jellyfish. Sometimes, such encounters can be painful as some species of jellyfish have poisonous tentacles that can sting the unwary swimmer. Other times, the encounter can be fatal. The box jellyfish, for example, is one of the world's most venomous creatures.

There are more than 200 species of jellyfish, close relatives to sea anemones and coral. Unlike coral, however, jellyfish are thriving because of changes in the climate and are rapidly moving into new habitats around the world as invasive species.

The explosion in jellyfish populations harms tourism and fishing industries worldwide. In 2007, giant jellyfish—weighing as much as 450 pounds—invaded the Sea of Japan, according to Madeleine Brand in an October 3, 2007 story on National Public Radio. In 2010 hundreds of swimmers at the South Carolina shore were stung by jellies, and beaches were closed along Spain's Mediterranean coast. In addition, a ten-year old Australian child barely survived her encounter with a box

(HABS) are plaguing ocean waters, particularly in coastal areas, as well as freshwater. Many scientists associate HABS with global warming.

Although as University of Tasmania professor Gustaaf Hallegraeff points out, "HABS in a strict sense are completely natural phenomena that occurred throughout recorded history," Such events contaminate water sources and have many ill effects on wildlife and humans.[12]

During a marine harmful algal bloom, sometimes known as a "red tide," shellfish take up the algae in the water and become contaminated. Marine creatures, birds, and humans who eat the contaminated shellfish sicken and may die. Red tides cause large

jellyfish, whose sting is usually fatal, according to science correspondent Ian Sample, writing in the April 27, 2010 issue of *The Guardian*.

Scientists attribute the success of the jellyfish to numerous factors. First, jellyfish have been inadvertently introduced to areas that have been overfished, such as the Black Sea. When there are adequate numbers of fish in a habitat, the small fish eat the jellyfish and keep their numbers in control. When there are fewer fish, the jellies eat the fish eggs and larvae, destroying their future predators.

Second, jellyfish can exploit low-oxygen areas of the ocean. Fertilizer runoff and global warming are causing, both directly and indirectly, ocean oxygen depletion, leading to the growth of so-called dead zones where most marine animals are unable to survive. Because jellies thrive in low-oxygen conditions, they can quickly overrun ocean habitats.

Third, as the climate changes and the ocean warms, jellyfish are able to reproduce more quickly. In addition, they are able to move into waters that were previously too cold for their survival. Thus, as suitable habitats for most marine creatures are shrinking, habitats suitable for jellies are growing. Indeed, researchers such as Anthony J. Richardson and Daniel Pauly, among many others, warn that the future of the ocean may belong to the jellyfish.

fish die-offs, and the dead fish then pose a health risk to more birds and other shore dwellers.

In Florida, for example, red tides are often the result of an organism that produces poisons known as "brevetoxins." According to Nancy Diersing of the Florida Keys National Marine Sanctuary, "The toxins produced in red tides can cause respiratory irritation in swimmers and marine animals and can make filter-feeding clams and oysters unfit for human consumption." Diersing also

---

Following pages: A red tide algal bloom spreads through a body of water in southeast Alaska. Algal overgrowth depletes the water of oxygen, killing some sea life. Jeff Foott/Discovery Channel Images/Getty Images.

writes that blooms affect the oxygen content of water in two ways: first, algae sometimes use up the available oxygen in the water; and second, once the bloom is over, the decomposition of the algae also removes oxygen from the water. "During some blooms, fish are seen gasping at the surface for oxygen and this lack of [oxygen] can be a direct cause of 'fish kills' observed on the scene."[13]

Another type of HABS affecting water quality and associated with global warming is that caused by the growth of cyanobacteria, usually found in fresh or brackish water. These blooms affect plants, fish, and other marine creatures in three ways, according to marine scientists Hans W. Paerl and Jeff Huisman: first, the blooms smother aquatic plants, thus destroying fish habitat; second, the blooms deplete oxygen levels; and third, the blooms may produce toxins causing illnesses and death among wildlife and humans.

HABS and Global Warming

Paerl and Huisman link cyanobacteria blooms with global warming and warn that "climate change is a potent catalyst for the further expansion of these blooms." The scientists make this claim based on evidence that cyanobacteria grow better in warmer water, suggesting that these organisms will crowd out other phytoplankton.[14]

Hallengraeff notes, "Prediction of the impact of global climate change on marine HABs is fraught with difficulties," largely because of the complex factors that interact to produce such a bloom. Nonetheless, he predicts that with climate change, the following can be expected: expanded ranges for warm-water species; poleward shifts in ranges of cold-water species; earlier appearance of blooms; and disruption of the oceanic food chain.[15]

Thus, it seems likely that in a warmer world, harmful algal blooms will occur more frequently and last longer. In addition, these blooms are likely to kill off many marine and freshwater species through habitat destruction and the contamination of water.

Acidification of the Ocean

One of the most alarming consequences of global warming for all life on the earth is the documented lowering of the ocean's pH levels as its waters become increasingly acidic. Scientists overwhelmingly agree that the acidification is growing, and that it

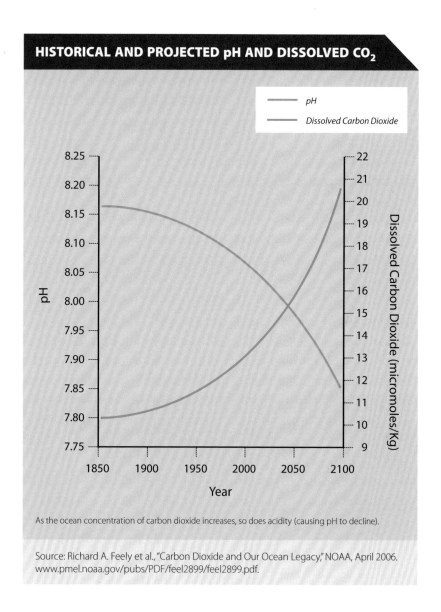

HISTORICAL AND PROJECTED pH AND DISSOLVED CO₂

pH

Dissolved Carbon Dioxide

As the ocean concentration of carbon dioxide increases, so does acidity (causing pH to decline).

Source: Richard A. Feely et al., "Carbon Dioxide and Our Ocean Legacy," NOAA, April 2006. www.pmel.noaa.gov/pubs/PDF/feel2899/feel2899.pdf.

is caused by the increased absorption of anthropogenic atmospheric CO_2. The ocean represents the most important carbon sink on the planet; oceanic uptake of CO_2 is a normal part of this role, but the increasingly high levels of CO_2 in the atmosphere are drastically changing ocean chemistry.

Changes in ocean chemistry can have a direct and catastrophic effect on organisms that live in the ocean. The acidification causes the shells of mollusks, crustaceans, and echinoderms to dissolve. In addition, the skeletons of fish also dissolve in water of sufficient acidity. Charlie Veron and Will Howard, scientists at the Antarctic Climate and Ecosystems Cooperative Research Center, expressed their grave concerns over ocean acidification in an interview with science journalist Graham Phillips in 2007. Veron, considered Australia's foremost coral reef expert, stated bluntly that ocean acidification "is the most serious problem of climate change. It is the big one."[16]

Corals, and their reefs, are also dissolving in areas of the ocean that have become acidic. According to marine biologist Ove Houegh-Guldberg and his research team, "Under conditions expected in the 21st century, global warming and ocean acidification will compromise carbonate accretion, with corals becoming increasingly rare on reef systems." Reefs are important habitats for many species, and they depend on the quality of water to support life. Houegh-Guldberg notes the complexity of the situation, suggesting that climate change makes all other factors affecting reef health worse: "Climate change also exacerbates local stresses from declining water quality and over exploitation of key species, driving reefs increasingly toward the tipping point of functional collapse."[17] Indeed, Veron predicts in an article in the London *Times*, "There is no way out, no loopholes. The Great Barrier Reef [in Australia] will be over within 20 years or so."[18]

Acidification of ocean waters leads to the acidification of the body fluids of many sea organisms. Such acidification of internal organs disrupts reproduction and other bodily functions. Scientists are also investigating the role that acidification of ocean water plays in changing the acoustical properties of seawater. Researchers Tatiana Ilyina, Richard E. Zeebe, and Peter G. Brewer have documented that the acidification of ocean water leads to less effective low-frequency sound absorption. They write,

> Sound absorption . . . could fall by up to 60% in the high latitudes and in areas of deep-water formation over the same time period. We predict that over the twenty-first century, chemical absorption of sound . . . will nearly halve in some regions that experience significant radiated noise from industrial activity, such as the North Atlantic Ocean.[19]

The failure of ocean water to absorb sound will make the seas noisier places. This change, in turn, can be linked to disruptions in marine mammal navigation. Ilyina notes that whales and dolpins may be affected by the higher noise levels. "The most extreme effects reported are tissue damage or mass stranding of whales associated with military tests of active acoustic systems."[20]

It is possible that the ocean will be the first large-scale catastrophe of global warming, leading to the complete collapse of the entire trophic, or food web, structure of the seas.

Scientists are viewing with growing dismay and alarm the implications of ocean acidification. It is possible that the ocean will be the first large-scale catastrophe of global warming, leading to the complete collapse of the entire trophic (food chain) structure of the seas. The tiny creatures of the sea, the plankton, echinoderms, and crustaceans, form the bottommost layer of the trophic structure. Howard argues that the death of these creatures due to ocean acidification "will have an ecological cascade effect right up to the parts of the food web that are important to human beings."[21] That is, without the bottom layer, all the layers above them collapse, from small fish, to sharks, to dolphins, to the mighty whales. It is possible that one day, all the seas of the world will be vast dead zones, unable to support life of any sort.

The Ocean as Carbon Sink

As noted above, the ocean is the most important carbon sink on the planet. As water temperatures warm, it is able to absorb less CO_2. There is also concern among many scientists that there may be a limit to how much carbon dioxide the ocean can absorb. Timothy Hall, for example, a physicist at NASA's Goddard Institute for Space Studies, describes his 2009 research which "suggests that the oceans are struggling to keep up with rising emissions." Furthermore, Hall and his colleagues have documented that there was a sharp increase of carbon absorption after 1950. The rate of increase seems to slow after 1980, however, and especially after 2000. Hall argues that this finding indicates "the fraction of anthropogenic CO_2 emissions entering the ocean seems to be slowing, even while the absolute tonnage increases. . . . The study suggests the slowdown is due to natural chemical limits on the ocean's ability to absorb carbon." He concludes that this evidence is "ominous," asserting that "a larger fraction of anthropogenic emissions will remain in the atmosphere, exacerbating the global warming due to industrial activity."[22]

This scenario is what scientists call a "positive feedback loop": Less absorption of carbon dioxide leads to warmer water temperatures. Warmer ocean waters lead to less absorption. Less absorption leads to even warmer water temperatures, and so on. In such a loop, the rate of increase generally accelerates. Although it is possible that some ocean wildlife will be able to adapt to the changes wrought by global warming, the accelerated rate of change may not make adaptation possible.

Notes

1. Richard Houghton, "Understanding the Global Carbon Cycle," Woods Hole Research Center, 2007. www.whrc.org.

2. US Environmental Protection Agency (EPA), "Ground-Level Ozone," March 8, 2010. www.epa.gov.

3. S. Sitch, "Indirective Radiative Forcing of Climate Change through Ozone Effects on the Land-Carbon Sink," *Nature*, vol. 448, August 17, 2007, p. 791.

4. US EPA , "What Is Acid Rain?" June 8, 2007. www.epa.gov.

5. Quoted in Amelia Apfel, "Acid Rain Is Not Only Changing Soil Chemistry, It Is Affecting Climate Change, Says Geological Survey Scientist," *ChronicleOnline*, Cornell University, January 30, 2008. www.news.cornell.edu.

6. Charles Driscoll and Larry O'Hanlon, "Interview: Acid Rain and Climate Change," *Discovery Earth*, May 25, 2009. dsc.discovery.com.

7. Jennifer Donovan, "Climate Change, Acid Rain Could Be Good for Forests," Michigan Tech News/Media, October 20, 2008. www.admin.mtu.edu.

8. Quoted in Robert Monroe and Mario Aguilera, "Oxygen Depletion: A New Form of Ocean Habitat Loss," Scripps Institution of Oceanography, May 1, 2008. www.eureka laert.org.

9. Les Blumenthal, "Worries Rise as Ocean Oxygen Levels Sink," *The Olympian* (Olympia, Washington), March 8, 2010. www.theolympian.com.

10. Quoted in Blumenthal, "Worries Rise as Ocean Oxygen Levels Sink."

11. Stephan Farris, "Jellyfish: A Gelantinous Invasion," *Time*, November 2, 2009. www .time.com.

12. Gustaaf M. Hallegraeff, "Ocean Climate Change, Phytoplankton Community Response, and Harmful Algal Blooms: A Formidable Predictive Challenge," *Journal of Phytocology*, vol. 46, no. 2, 2010, p. 220.

13. Nancy Diersing, "Phytoplankton Blooms," Florida Keys National Marine Sanctuary, May 2009. floridakeys.noaa.gov.

14. Hans W. Paerl and Jef Huismain, "Blooms Like It Hot," *Science*, vol. 320, April 4, 2008, p. 57.

15. Hallegraeff, "Ocean Climate Change, Phytoplankton Community Response, and Harmful Algal Blooms," p. 2002.

16. Graham Phillips, Charlie Veron, and Will Howard, "Interview: Ocean Acidification—the BIG Global Warming Story," *Catalyst*, Australian Broadcasting System, September 13, 2007. www.abc.net.au.

17. Ove Hoegh-Guldberg et al., "Coral Reefs Under Rapid Climate Change and Ocean Acidification," *Science*, vol. 318, December 14, 2007, p. 1737.

18. Quoted in Frank Pope, "Great Barrier Reef Will Be Gone in 20 Years, Says Charlie Veron," *Times OnLine*, July 7, 2009. www.timesonline.co.uk.

19. Tatiana Ilyina, Richard E. Zeebe, and Peter G. Brewer, "Future Ocean Increasingly Transparent to Low-Frequency Sound Owing to Carbon Dioxide Emissions," *Nature Geoscience*, vol. 3, 2010, p. 18.

20. Quoted in *Ecologist*, "Marine Mammals Under Threat from Ocean Noise Pollution," December 21, 2009. www.theecologist.org.

21. Phillips, "Interview."

22. Timothy Hall, "Can Ocean Carbon Uptake Keep Pace with Industrial Emissions?" Goddard Institute for Space Studies, December 2009. www.giss.nasa.gov.

CHAPTER 7

Global Warming, Mass Extinctions, and Biodiversity

Biologists David B. Wake and Vance T. Vredenburg note, "There have been five great mass extinctions during the history of life on this planet. . . . The possibility that a sixth mass extinction spasm is upon us has received much attention. Substantial evidence suggests that an extinction event is under way."[1] Strong evidence suggests that Wake and Vredenburg are correct in their analysis. The rate of species extinctions is accelerating rapidly; although scientists have many hypotheses about the reasons, there seems to be a link between extinctions and rapid climate change.

Past Climate Change

Many people are familiar with periods in the earth's history that resulted in mass extinctions; perhaps the best known is the extinction of the dinosaurs. Many other creatures and plants that once lived on the planet no longer exist, however. The only knowledge of these organisms comes through fossils, bones, and sedimentary evidence. There are many hypotheses to explain the causes of prehistoric and historic extinctions, including climate change.

Paleoclimatology is a field of science that examines past climate change and provides important information regarding extinctions in the past. In addition, examining past climate change may offer evidence for the causes and effects of present-day global warming.

Before the industrial revolution of the eighteenth century, the main drivers of climate change, according to the US Environmental Protection Agency, were

- Changes in the earth's orbit. These processes take place over a timescale of tens to hundreds of millennia.
- Changes in the sun's intensity. Changes in solar output can happen over centuries. For example, from the fifteenth century through the eighteenth century, there was a noticeable cooling of North America and Europe, probably caused by a reduction in solar output.
- Volcanic eruptions. Volcanoes can affect the climate in two opposite ways: First, aerosol emissions, or ash clouds, can block sunlight and cause temporary cooling. Second, carbon dioxide emissions introduce greenhouse gas into the atmosphere, leading to warming. Since the eighteenth century, however, according to the EPA, "While volcanoes may have raised prehistoric CO_2 levels and temperatures . . . human activities now emit 150 times as much CO_2 as volcanoes (whose emissions are relatively modest compared to some earlier times . . .)."[2]

Gradual Versus Abrupt Climate Change

It was previously thought that the earth's climate changed gradually and slowly, over millennia and longer. As paleoclimatologist Peter U. Clark and his fellow researchers report, however, "Evidence pieced together over the last few decades . . . shows that climate has changed much more rapidly—sometimes abruptly—in the past and therefore could do it again." Some of this evidence derives from research on the Younger Dryas cold interval. This interval was brief, on a geologic scale: It lasted slightly more than 1,000 years, beginning about 12,800 years ago. Perhaps most notable about the Younger Dryas, however, is that it began and ended very abruptly, according to Clark. In investigating the Younger Dryas, Clark and his team discovered through an examination of "110,000-year-long ice-core records from Greenland and other climate records" that the "Younger Dryas was one in a long string of abrupt climate changes."[3]

Scientists hypothesize that such events occur either because of some sudden occurrence, such as a gigantic meteor strike or massive volcanism; or because of many other drivers, working in concert, that push the earth's climate system to a tipping point. As the drivers are forcing the system, the change may be negligible. Once the tipping point is reached, however, the climate can change rapidly and with little warning. Abrupt climate change may result in the extinction of many species, as organisms lack sufficient time to adapt to the new environmental conditions.

Climate Change and Past Extinction Events

Extinction events are probably caused by a combination of factors working together synergistically. It is, therefore, very difficult to determine why some species decline and others endure. Recent research methods have shed light on previously little-understood events, however.

For example, some of the most puzzling and interesting extinctions occurred during the Pleistocene epoch, a period of the earth's history that began about 2.588 million years before the present and lasted until about 12,000 years before the present (the late years of the Pleistocene epoch coincide with the Younger Dryas). The end of the Pleistocene marks one of the earth's great extinction events. As science writer Brian Switek notes, "Of all the mass extinctions that have occurred during [the] earth's history, among the most hotly debated is the one which wiped out mammoths, saber-toothed cats, giant ground sloths, and the other peculiar members of the Pleistocene megafauna around 12,000 years ago."[4]

What Caused the Pleistocene Extinctions?

Indeed, the mass extinctions of the Pleistocene have been shrouded in mystery. There are, however, two elements char-

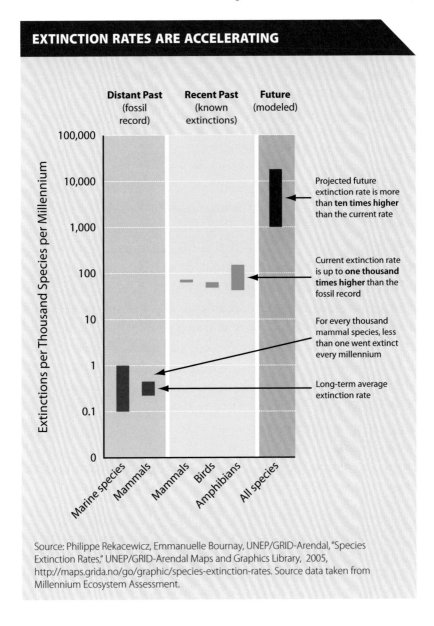

EXTINCTION RATES ARE ACCELERATING

Source: Philippe Rekacewicz, Emmanuelle Bournay, UNEP/GRID-Arendal, "Species Extinction Rates," UNEP/GRID-Arendal Maps and Graphics Library, 2005, http://maps.grida.no/go/graphic/species-extinction-rates. Source data taken from Millennium Ecosystem Assessment.

acteristic of the last years of the epoch that seem to offer some linkage with the extinction event: first, it was a period of rapid climate change; and second, humans were beginning to spread across the northern hemisphere. In addition, though creatures such as mammoths and woolly rhinoceroses did not survive, others—such as bison, horses, and caribou—did.

If the earth is indeed in the spasms of a sixth mass extinction, many of the life forms presently alive will no longer exist in the future.

"The reasons for these drastically different survival patterns have been widely debated," notes biologist Beth Shapiro, "with some scientists claiming that the extinctions were due largely to human hunting." Shapiro points to the "unique opportunity" to examine the evidence represented by arctic musk oxen. The beasts were plentiful during the Pleistocene, but now only a remnant endures, all living in Greenland. By studying the DNA of oxen from bones dated from as much as 60,000 years ago and comparing it with DNA from present-day herds, Shapiro and her colleagues were able to estimate declines in genetic diversity indicating a reduction in population. As a result, they could then "test whether the decline was due to the arrival of human beings in a particular region or to some other effect." Through careful analysis of their data, the researchers determined that climate change was most likely the cause of arctic musk oxen decline. Shapiro concludes,

> We know from historical data that musk oxen are sensitive to changes in the Arctic environment. . . . While we cannot confirm exactly what climate factors are driving the changes we observe in musk oxen over the last 65,000 years, we can say with confidence that humans are not causing local extinctions.[5]

The Causes of Present-Day Extinctions

The present day is a time of great biodiversity when compared to the past, yet it appears that this biodiversity is threatened by a host of factors. If the earth is indeed in the spasms of a sixth mass extinction, many of the life forms presently alive will no longer exist in the future.

Jared Diamond, in his now-famous chapter "Overview of Recent Extinctions" in *Conservation for the Twenty-First Century*, listed the circumstances that underpin most modern extinctions, calling them the "Evil Quartet."[6] Diamond identifies four key ecological traits associated with extinctions: overkill, habitat loss and fragmentation, invasive or introduced species, and cascades of extinctions or coextinctions. Although many scientists agree with Diamond's assessment, others argue that other equally compelling reasons for extinctions exist, and that many of the factors he notes are exacerbated by climate change. Biologist Robert R. Dunn and his fellow researchers, for example, argue that climate change ought to be added as a "fifth horseman."[7]

The Connection Between Global Warming and Extinctions

Biologist Camille Parmesan agrees. This University of Texas professor of integrative biology reviewed more than 800 studies on the effects of anthropogenic global climate change on wildlife. What she found confirms that climate change is taking a toll on many species. The results of her study demonstrate that "the most sensitive species are going extinct and/or shifting their ranges geographically as their original habitats become inhospitable." She also notes that "pests and diseases are also showing the same northward shifts as other animals,"[8] suggesting that more wildlife could be subject to increased problems with both disease and blight.

Parmesan's study reveals that habitat loss and fragmentation can be partially attributed to global warming at the same time that other factors may interact to amplify and worsen the situation. The case of the golden toad serves as an example of complexity. For a number of years, scientists believed that the extinction of this amphibian was due to climate change. After more research, however, a much murkier picture emerges. The

1999 extinction is probably due to a host of causes, rather than to global warming alone. Nevertheless, the golden toad also serves as an illustration of how the impact of global warming on an already tenuous existence can be the tipping point that pushes a species from marginal viability into extinction.

Some researchers, however, have been able to link predictions of a species' extinction directly with global warming. Studies such as those of biologist Barry Sinervo and his research team provide the data needed to make such linkages. In their study of forty-eight species of lizards at two-hundred sites in Mexico, the team was able to decisively conclude that 12 percent of the species were "locally extinct by 2009." The cause of the lizards' decline was hot weather. Although lizards need solar heat to survive, if the temperatures climb too high, the lizards can overheat and die. Lizards cope with high temperatures by finding shelter and resting in shady or cooler places. If they are not able to forage actively for food during increasing hours of the day, however, they will be unable to grow or reproduce. In short, the change of maximum air temperatures in Mexico is leading to lizard death by starvation. The research team concludes, "Probability of local extinction is projected to result in species extinction of 6% by 2050 and 20% by 2080."[9] The significance of the team's findings is further emphasized by an accompanying editorial. Biologist Raymond Huey, and zoologists Jonathan B. Losos and Craig R. Moritz applaud the methods and findings of Sinervo et al., stating, "Global warming is expected to drive widespread extinctions, but predictions are rarely validated against actual extinctions and by knowledge of causal mechanisms. Sinervo et al. deliver a disturbing message: Climate-forced extinctions are not only in the future but are happening now."[10]

Mammals, Climate Change, and Extinction

Many other species are disappearing from the earth. Mammals, in particular, are in danger of extinction. Indeed, of all mammals for which adequate data are available, fully 25 percent of them

The western fence lizard (Sceloporus occidentalis) is one of the species that has disappeared from several sites in Mexico due to changes in desert temperatures. Rich Reid/National Geographic/Getty Images.

are in danger of extinction, according to conservation biologist Jan Schipper and his fellow researchers.

Schipper writes, "The conservation status of marine species is of particular concern with an estimated 36% (range, 23[%] to 61%) of species threatened." Schipper's study reveals that the gravest danger to marine mammals is derived from accidental death, largely through interaction with fishing vessels. Yet, 60 percent of marine mammals are affected by pollution, a designation that "includes a diversity of mechanisms, such as chemical contaminants, marine debris, noise, and climate change. Sound pollution (military sonar) has been implicated in mass strandings of cetaceans, and climate change is already [affecting] sea-ice dependent species," such as the polar bear and harp seal. The most endangered mammals tend to live in Asia and to have a lengthy life span and a large body size. Tigers, tapirs, and hippos are particularly good examples. Schipper's survey of the earth's mammals concludes that "one in four species is threatened with extinction and that the population of one in two is declining."[11]

Birds in Danger

As a group, birds are among the most endangered of all animals. A stunning 400 of the world's 8,750 bird species are in serious danger of extinction, primarily because of loss of habitat and global warming, according to science writer Mark Clayton, reporting on a 2007 study conducted by the National Audubon Society. The study reveals that some species, such as crows, doves, and robins, are spending their winters farther north.

From the Brink of Extinction: Kirtland's Warbler

Kirtland's warblers are exceedingly rare. They nest on the ground in young stands of jack pines, largely in northern Lower Michigan. According to the US Fish and Wildlife Service, the trees must be five to twenty feet tall and six to twenty-two years old. In addition, warblers require sandy soil with good drainage. Warblers also need at least 8 acres (3.2 ha) to nest and an additional 30–40 acres (12–16 ha) to fledge their young.

The population of approximately 1,000 warblers counted in 1961 plummeted to just 400 individuals by 1971, after having been listed as endangered in 1967. It seemed likely that the bird was headed for extinction.

Kirtland's warblers had two major problems. Jack pines reproduce only as the result of forest fires that cause jack pine cones to release their seed. Years of forest-fire suppression had prevented new-growth jack pine forests. In addition, the brown-headed cowbird, an invasive species, practices nest parasitism on the warblers by laying its eggs in the warblers' nests. Cowbird young are bigger and hatch earlier than warbler nestlings, and the cowbirds can cause the baby warblers' deaths.

In 1973, the Michigan Department of Natural Resources, the US

These species do not appear to be in trouble. Nonetheless, as Clayton writes,

> Other species that rely on cold climates, like the snow bunting and greater scaup, which breed in Alaskan and Canadian tundra, are showing signs of trouble. As the tundra warms, it cedes to shrubs unsuitable for birds to breed. . . . Scaup numbers are down 75 percent and bunting [are down] 64 percent, in part because these species can't go farther north to breed.[12]

Furthermore, global warming acts synergistically in placing birds in peril of extinction.

Geological Survey, the US Forest Service, and the US Fish and Wildlife Service banded together to help save the warblers from extinction. Public lands have been set aside, and managers regularly create new, suitable habitat for the bird: They clear-cut forests, and plant jack pine seeds each year. They have also undertaken a cowbird eradication policy in the managed lands.

In 2008, the Kirtland's warbler population numbered more than 1,800 individuals, 94 percent of them on managed lands in Michigan. Although this story demonstrates how a species can be saved from extinction through concerted conservation efforts, the future of Kirtland's warblers is far from certain.

Global warming may be the final factor in the warblers' demise. According to Terry L. Root and Stephen H. Schneider, jack pines "will move north with warming, but the warbler is not likely to survive the transition." The soil farther north in Michigan is not sandy enough to meet habitat requirements for nesting. Root and Schneider conclude, "Consequently, global warming could well doom the warbler to extinction in 30 to 60 years. This potential for extinction indicates how the already high rate of extinctions around the world could be exacerbated by climatic changes, occurring more rapidly than species can adapt."*

*Terry L. Root and Stephen H. Schneider, "Climate Change: Overview and Implications for Wildlife," *Wildlife Responses to Climate Change: North American Case Studies*, Washington, DC: Island Press, 2002, p. 3.

The case of the cuckoo, a bird once common in England and Scotland, illustrates the complexity of factors involved in potential extinctions. The cuckoo summers in Britain but spends winters in sub-Saharan Africa. This area has experienced extreme drought and desertification in recent decades, making it difficult for the birds to find adequate food and water in their wintering grounds. In addition, butterflies are among the cuckoo's preferred foods, and the worldwide decline of butterflies has also decreased the availability of food for the cuckoo. Moreover, cuckoos lay their eggs in the nests of other birds, notably the meadow pipit and the dunnock. These birds are also in decline, leading to fewer nests and fewer opportunities for the cuckoo to lay eggs. Finally, as climate change and human encroachment affect forests, the cuckoo's primary habitat is becoming increasingly fragmented, leading to further endangerment and risk of extinction. The decline in the cuckoo population is both rapid and marked: According to environmental correspondent David Adam, writing in the May 28, 2009 issue of *The Guardian*, cuckoos have lost 37 percent of their population since the mid-1990s. Clearly, the intertwined and self-amplifying problems the cuckoo experiences in its struggle for viability as a species demonstrate how complicated and complex the process of survival can become. As the National Audubon Society concludes, "Whether they have already shifted their ranges or are unable to do so, bird species illustrate how the impact of global warming compounds other well-known threats."[13]

The Rapid Rate of Amphibian Extinctions

Amphibians, however, may represent the first, large-scale mass extinction that can be attributed at least in part to global warming. There are, at present, only 6,200 living species of amphibians, and a growing number of scientists fear for the animals' future. Wake and Vredenburg report, "Amphibians have received much attention during the last two decades because of a now-general understanding that a larger proportion of amphibian species are [*sic*] at risk of extinction than those of any other taxon."[14] Fossils indicate that in the distant past, far more amphibians existed than do today. Indeed, amphibian species were much more successful in the geologic past than they have been in the modern era. It is likely that reptiles and mammals posed significant competition for these creatures and pushed many species into extinction.

Yet in the present, amphibians are in crisis because of habitat loss and fragmentation; degraded water quality; sensitivity to temperature changes; emerging new diseases; and introduction of exotic species. Wake and Vredenburg place the blame squarely on human beings:

> Perhaps the most profound impact [on amphibians] is the human role in climate change, the effects of which may have been small so far, but which will shortly be dramatic. . . . Multiple factors acting synergistically are contributing to the loss of amphibians. But we can be sure that behind all of these activities is one weedy species, *Homo sapiens*.[15]

The Case for Conservation: Protecting Biodiversity on Planet Earth

The threat of extinction extends over many species of plants and wildlife, around the globe. Climate change, caused by humans, is pushing many species over the brink. Consequently, humans must undertake conservation measures and habitat protection in order to prevent as many extinctions as possible. Doing so is important in order to preserve biodiversity on the planet.

Why is biodiversity so important? According to the Australian Academy of Science, there are many reasons: "Biodiversity increases the ability of ecosystems to do things like hold soils together, maintain soil fertility, deliver clean water to streams and rivers, cycle nutrients, pollinate plants (including crops) and buffer against pests and diseases." All of these so-called "ecosystem functions" are integral to the global food web. Furthermore, monoculture, the farming of one crop as opposed to many, is vulnerable to both pest and disease. A single microorganism can wipe out an entire economy if it attacks the lone crop on which that economy rests. The nineteenth-century Irish potato famine offers a frightening example of how a blight can lead to untold suffering and death. In sum, according to the Australian Academy of Science, the loss of biodiversity could mean "land degradation, changes in agricultural productivity and a reduction in the quality of water delivered to human populations."[16] These outcomes are not limited to humans. All of nature and all wildlife suffers when a species is lost.

Moreover, researchers such as biologist Steve Ormerod and Isabelle Durance have demonstrated that even tiny organisms have a role to play in ecosystem integrity. Their work centers on three small snails found in the grasslands of southeastern England. Although it is easy to scoff at special conservation plans aimed at protecting snails, Ormerod and Durance have demonstrated that conserving snails has a large impact on the surrounding areas. Ormerod writes, "Sites set aside and managed for the snails turn out not only to be unique and special places that protect other species, but also have the best quality—for example, with the cleanest water."[17] That is, the effort to conserve the snails has resulted in an improved environment for all creatures living in the area. As Durance adds, "The evidence about the wider benefits and value of conserving rare invertebrates comes at a critical time. . . . Just how well we protect the world's biodiversity is a key indicator of whether we're managing our environment in a truly sustainable way."[18]

These studies and others suggest the inherent value of each species on the earth. Even though humans tend to think in terms of what benefits them, it is important for everyone to develop a more global, interspecies perspective. If the earth is truly an interconnected web of life, what damages one thread of the web damages the entire planetary system.

Notes

1. David B. Wake and Vance T. Vredenberg, "Are We in the Midst of the Sixth Mass Extinction? A View from the World of Amphibians," *Proceedings of the National Academy of Sciences*, vol. 108, August 12, 2008, p. 11466.
2. US Environmental Protection Agency, "Past Climate Change," *Climate Change Science*, September 28, 2009. www.epa.gov.
3. Peter U. Clark et al., "Abrupt Climate Change: Inevitable Surprises," *Abrupt Climate Change: A Report by the US Climate Change Science Program and the Subcommittee on Global Change Research*, 2008. www.climatescience.gov.
4. Brian Switek, "Prehistoric DNA Reveals the Story of a Pleistocene Survivor, the Muskox," *Laelaps*, March 10, 2010. scienceblogs.com/laelaps/about.php.
5. Quoted in *Penn State Live*, "Musk Ox Population Decline Due to Climate, Not to Humans, Study Finds," Pennsylvania State University, March 9, 2010. live.psu.edu.
6. Jared Diamond, "Overview of Recent Extinctions," *Conservation for the Twenty-First Century*, eds. David Western and Mary C. Pearl, New York: Wildlife Conservation International, 1989, pp. 37–41.
7. Robert R. Dunn et al., "The Sixth Mass Coextinction: Are Most Endangered Species Parasites and Mutualists?" *Proceedings of the Royal Society: Biological Sciences*, vol. 276, no. 1670, p. 3307.
8. Quoted in Lee Clippard, "Global Warming Increases Species Extinctions Worldwide, University of Texas Austin Researcher Finds," University of Texas at Austin, November 14, 2006. www.utexas.edu.
9. Barry Sinervo et al., "Erosion of Lizard Diversity by Climate Change and Altered Thermal Niches," *Science*, vol. 328, May 14, 2010, p. 894.
10. Raymond B. Huey, Jonathan B. Losos, and Craig Moritz, "Are Lizards Toast?" *Science*, vol. 328, May 14, 2010, p. 832.
11. Jan Schipper et al., "The Status of the World's Land and Marine Mammals: Diversity, Threat and Knowledge," *Science*, vol. 322, pp. 228–30.
12. Mark Clayton, "Common Bird Species in Dramatic Decline," *Christian Science Monitor*, June 15, 2007. www.csmonitor.com.
13. National Audubon Society, "Birds and Climate Change: Ecological Disruption in Motion," February 2009. www.audubon.org.
14. Wake, "Are We in the Midst of the Sixth Mass Extinction? A View from the World of Amphibians," p. 11467.
15. Wake, "Are We in the Midst of the Sixth Mass Extinction? A View from the World of Amphibians," p. 11472.
16. Australian Academy of Science, "Impact of Global Warming on Biodiversity," *Nova: Science in the News*, October 2005. www.science.org.au.
17. Steve Ormerod, "Sustainability Week," Cardiff University, 2010, www.cardiff.ac.uk/sustainability/week/newinsights/articles/steve-ormerod.html.
18. Quoted in Ormerod, "Sustainability Week."

CHAPTER 8

The Impact of Global Warming on Nature and Wildlife: Conclusion

The interplay of nature and wildlife with global warming is dauntingly complex. Although science has been successful in gathering evidence and data to provide working answers to the questions raised by global warming, many hypotheses remain to be tested. Only through methodical testing and careful analysis will answers to the tough questions of climate change emerge. Biologist Raymond B. Huey and zoologists Jonathan B. Losos and Craig Moritz argue that "an effective framework for exploring organismal susceptibility to climate change" should include "documenting extinctions, evaluating underlying biophysical and eco-physiological mechanisms, considering the potential for adaptive evasion, and then building projection models based explicitly on established mechanisms."[1] Only through careful attention to the scientific method will sufficient data and evidence be gathered to establish the validity of global warming projections.

The synergism of climate change, habitat destruction, and pollution make it difficult to single out climate change as the causal factor in declines and extinctions in nature and among wildlife. In spite of the difficulty, however, research continues to indicate that there are strong links between climate change and damage to nature and wildlife. A study of lizard extinctions in Mexico, undertaken by Barry Sinervo and his large research team, has succeeded in directly attributing the extinction of twelve percent of local lizard populations to rising temperatures, for example.

Adaptation and Abrupt Climate Change

Some plants and animals seem to have already begun to adapt to the changing climate. As temperatures have increased, some plants and animals have begun to shift their habitats toward the poles, or to higher altitudes, in order to remain within a range of temperatures needed for their survival. Other species have adjusted their phenology, or life cycles, to respond to earlier springs and longer summers, or to warmer winters. Indeed, ample evidence exists that, over long periods of time, many species will be able to adapt to changes in the climate.

It appears that the earth may be experiencing what can only be called "abrupt" climate change, however. Temperatures may increase over decades, rather than over centuries. The weather experienced by a given region may become rapidly more violent. Such abrupt changes do not give species enough time to adapt, and many species may be lost to extinction.

Mitigating the Impact of Global Warming on Nature and Wildlife

Humans can help preserve nature and wildlife from some of the impact of global warming. Although it may not be possible to fully curb temperature increases, humans can nevertheless minimize some of the effects. As researcher Barry W. Brook and his colleagues point out, however, "Conservation actions which only target single-threat drivers risk being inadequate because of the cascading effects of unmanaged synergies."[2] In other words, conservation efforts must take into account the many interacting factors leading to a species' decline.

High on the list of possible mitigation strategies is a concentration on habitat conservation. At the same time that global warming contributes to habitat loss and fragmentation, human encroachment on plant and animal habitats is also a great danger. By limiting this encroachment, and thereby allowing habitats to remain contiguous rather than fragmented, people can help some species avoid endangerment and extinction.

Reducing carbon emissions worldwide will also mitigate climate change. Although it seems clear that temperatures will continue to increase, the rate of increase can be slowed. Furthermore, reducing carbon emissions will also help to slow the acidification of the ocean. Finally, reducing carbon emissions will reduce pollution in urban areas, thus preventing spillover pollution from reaching more rural and wild environments.

At the same time, it is important for planners to consider the ways that reducing carbon emissions might affect nature and wildlife. For example, wind farms hold the promise for abundant and clean energy, with none of the carbon emissions typical of coal-burning power plants. If wind farms are constructed in the flight paths of migratory birds, however, the facilities could cause the destruction of entire species. Likewise, although nuclear power plants provide so-called clean energy, an accident at such a plant could render the surrounding area completely devoid of all life for centuries.

A Commitment to Biodiversity

At a fundamental level, one of the most important contributions human beings can make to planet Earth is to develop a commitment to biodiversity. Only through an understanding of the importance of biodiversity for all can humans be able and willing to protect and preserve nature and wildlife in a warming world. As writer Brian Walsh reflects,

> In a world where hundreds of millions of human beings still go hungry and the global recession has left all but the wealthiest fearing for their future, it's easy to wonder why we should be concerned about the dwindling of the planet's biodiversity. The answer is that we can't afford not to. The same natural qualities that sustain wildlife . . . ultimately sustain us as well,

whether we live in a green jungle or a concrete one. But there is an innate value to untrammeled biodiversity too—one that goes beyond our own survival. When that is lost, we are irretrievably diminished.[3]

Notes

1. Raymond B. Huey, Jonathan B. Losos, and Craig Moritz, "Are Lizards Toast?" *Science,* vol. 328, May 14, 2010, p. 833.
2. Barry W. Brook, "Synergies Among Extinction Drivers Under Global Change," *Trends in Ecology and Evolution,* vol. 23, issue 8, August 2008, p. 453.
3. Bryan Walsh, "The New Age of Extinction," *Time,* April 13, 2009, p. 43.

Glossary

acidification The process of becoming more acidic; in the case of the ocean, acidification occurs through the absorption of carbon dioxide gas.

anthropogenic Caused by humans.

arable Land that is suitable for growing crops.

biodiversity Variety of life in the world or in a particular habitat.

carbon dioxide (CO_2) A greenhouse gas chemically composed of carbon and oxygen. Carbon dioxide is produced by the burning of fossil fuels such as oil and coal. It is also exhaled by human beings and inhaled by plants. Burning plants also release carbon dioxide.

chytrid fungus A fungus that causes a fatal disease among amphibians.

coral bleaching The process of the whitening of coral, caused by the stress-induced expulsion or death of algae living in symbiosis with the coral.

cyanobacteria Blue-green algae producing toxic substances that can pose significant danger to wildlife and humans.

desertification The gradual process of habitable land turning into desert as a result of climate change or poor farming practices.

drought A long period of abnormally low rainfall, especially one that affects growing or living conditions.

eutrophication Excessive nutrients in lakes or ponds causing an excess of plant and algal growth, often leading to oxygen depletion and "dead zones" where animals can no longer live.

feedback loop A process in which one condition creates other conditions that reinforce the first.

glacier A mass of ice that is located year-round on, and that moves over, land.

global warming The increase in the average temperature of the earth's surface and the ocean. Global warming has been occurring since the mid-twentieth century and is expected to continue because of the greenhouse effect.

greenhouse effect The heating of the surface of the earth due to the presence of atmospheric gases that trap energy from the sun.

greenhouse gases Substances that contribute to the greenhouse effect and global warming. Carbon dioxide, methane, and water vapor are all greenhouse gases.

habitat The natural home or environment of an animal or plant.

habitat fragmentation The breakup of a habitat into smaller, noncontiguous parts; caused by climate change, natural disaster, or human incursion, among other causes.

heat wave A prolonged period of abnormally hot weather.

Intergovernmental Panel on Climate Change (IPCC) A scientific body established by the United Nations to evaluate the risk of climate change caused by human activity.

ozone A gas consisting of three oxygen atoms. In the stratosphere, ozone protects the earth from harmful radiation; in the troposphere, ozone is a dangerous pollutant causing serious human illness and distress.

paleoclimatology The study of climates in the geologic past.

phenology The study of cyclic and seasonal phenomena, particularly in relation to climate, plants, and wildlife.

seawater incursion Contamination of rivers, lakes, and reservoirs with saltwater that makes the freshwater undrinkable and unusable for irrigation; often caused by storms or floods.

smog A combination of smoke, particulates, and fog.

storm surge A rapid rise in offshore ocean water, resulting in shoreline flooding and occurring during a tropical cyclone or hurricane; caused by high winds pushing water toward shore, combined with an ocean-level rise due to low atmospheric pressure at the storm center.

symbiosis Interaction between two living organisms, living in close physical association, usually to the benefit of both.

synergy The interaction of two or more agents or processes to produce a combined effect greater than the sum of their individual effects.

trophic structure The relationship of an organism to other organisms in terms of the food web; sometimes called the food chain, it is better thought of as an interconnected web.

ultraviolet radiation Invisible rays that are part of the energy from the sun; can cause sunburn and various kinds of skin cancer.

urban heat island A metropolitan area that is significantly warmer than surrounding rural areas because of the number of paved surfaces and buildings, which typically absorb heat rather than reflect it.

vector-borne disease Infectious illness caused by the bite of another organism, such as a tick or mosquito.

water-borne illness Disease caused by exposure to or consumption of water contaminated by pathogenic microorganisms.

wetlands Areas of land whose soil is saturated with moisture, either permanently or seasonally.

zoonotic disease An animal disease, such as rabies, that can be spread to humans.

For Further Research

Books

David Archer, *The Global Carbon Cycle*. Princeton, NJ:
Princeton University Press, 2010.
> A short introduction to the carbon cycle; includes a glossary, explanation of equations, suggestions for further reading, and a discussion of how the global carbon cycle is an integral part of the earth's climate system.

———, *The Long Thaw: How Humans Are Changing the Next 100,000 Years of Earth's Climate*. Princeton, NJ: Princeton University Press, 2009.
> In a conversational style, Archer explains the current picture of climate change, and what can be expected in the coming decades, centuries, and millennia.

Anthony D. Barnosky, *Heat Stroke: Nature in an Age of Global Warming*. Washington, DC: Island Press, 2009.
> An examination by a paleoclimatologist of the way abrupt climate change is affecting animals, connecting the present situation to events in the earth's past.

Gary Braasch, *Earth Under Fire: How Global Warming Is Changing the World*, 2nd ed. Berkeley, CA: University of California Press, 2009.
> An illustrated account of how global warming is changing the planet.

Jonathan Cowans, *Climate Change: Biological and Human Aspects*. Cambridge, UK: Cambridge University Press, 2007.
> Examines past, present, and future climate change from biological and ecological points of view, offering an assessment of the impact of global warming on wildlife as well as on humans.

Stephan Faris, *Forecast: The Surprising—and Immediate—Consequences of Climate Change*. New York: Holt, 2009.
> A travel journalist visits places around the world to report on the effects of climate change, including the impact on wildlife and nature.

Fred Granath and Mirielle de la Lez, *Vanishing World: The Endangered Arctic*. New York: Abrams, 2007.
> Illustrated with many photographs, this book details the existence of wildlife in the harsh Arctic environment and what is at risk because of global warming.

Colin A. Hunt, *Carbon Sinks and Climate Change: Forests in the Fight Against Global Warming*. Northampton, MA: Edward Elgar, 2009.
> Argues that forests can be an effective tool in reducing the amount of greenhouse gases released into the atmosphere.

Craig Idso, *CO2, Global Warming and Coral Reefs*. Pueblo West, CO: Vales Lake, 2009.
> An investigation of the effects of carbon dioxide on global warming and of ocean acidification on coral reefs.

Michael C. MacCracken, Frances Moore, and John C. Copping, *Sudden and Disruptive Climate Change: Exploring the Real Risks and How We Can Avoid Them*. London: Earthscan, 2008.
> An international group of scientists considers the evidence that climate change may not be slow and gradual but, instead, abrupt; they examine the Greenland ice sheet, extreme rain events, and coastal inundation.

Michael E. Mann and Lee R. Kump, *Dire Predictions: Understanding Global Warming*. New York: DK, 2008.
> Two leading climate scientists provide a clear explanation of the findings of the Intergovernmental Panel on Climate Change (IPCC), with ample illustrations and graphics.

Mark Maslin, *Global Warming: Causes, Effects, and the Future*. Stillwater, MN: Voyageur, 2007.
> An easily understood overview of global warming and its impact on health, agriculture, water, forests, and wildlife.

Gavin Schmidt et al., *Climate Change: Picturing the Science*. New York: Norton, 2009.
> Discusses increases in drought, forest fires, and extreme weather attributable to global warming; includes illustrations and photographs.

Siegfried Fred Singer and Dennis T. Avery, *Unstoppable Global Warming: Every 1,500 Years.* Lanham, MD: Rowan and Littlefield, 2007.
> Argues that global warming is part of an unstoppable natural process that does little harm.

S. Solomon et al., *Climate Change 2007: The Physical Science Basis.* Cambridge, UK: Cambridge University Press, 2007.
> A publication of the Intergovernmental Panel on Climate Change, covering historical and contemporary data on surface and atmospheric climate change.

Periodicals

Margie Beilharz, "Climate Change Raises the Disease Threat," *Ecos*, December 2008.

Christian Both, "Flexibility of Timing of Avian Migration to Climate Change Masked by Environmental Constraints En Route," *Current Biology*, vol. 20, no. 3, February 9, 2010.

Peter G. Brewer and James Barry, "Rising Acidity in the Ocean: The Other CO_2 Problem," *Scientific American*, October 7, 2008.

Ana D. Davidson et al., "Multiple Ecological Pathways to Extinction in Mammals," *PNAS* 106, no. 26, June 30, 2009.

Spencer R. Hall et al., "Warmer Does Not Have to Mean Sicker: Temperature and Predators Can Jointly Drive Timing of Epidemics," *Ecology*, vol. 87, no. 7, 2006.

G.C. Hays, A.J. Richardson, and C. Robinson, "Climate Change and Marine Plankton," *Trends in Ecology and Evolution*, vol. 20, no. 6, 2005.

Toke T. Høye et al., "Rapid Advancement of Spring in the High Arctic." *Current Biology*, vol. 17, no. 12, June 19, 2007.

Thomas H. Maugh II, "Lizards Face Extinction Because of Global Warming, Study Finds," *Los Angeles Times*, May 13, 2010.

David Morrison, "Did a Cosmic Impact Kill the Mammoths?" *Skeptical Inquirer*, May–June 2010.

News RX Health & Science, "'Deadly Dozen' Reports Diseases Worsened by Climate Change," October 26, 2008.

Mark W. Schwartz et al., "Predicting Extinctions as a Result of Climate Change," *Ecology*, vol. 87, no. 7, 2006.

Raman Sukumar, "Forest Research for the 21st Century," *Science* 13, no. 5882, June 13, 2008.

J.E.N. Veron et al., "The Coral Reef Crisis: The Critical Importance of <350 ppm CO_2," *Marine Pollution Bulletin* 58, 2009.

Internet Sources

Rhett A. Butler, "Global Warming May Cause Biodiversity Extinction," *MongaBay.com*, March 21, 2007. news .mongabay.com.

Defenders of Wildlife, "Impacts of Global Warming on Wildlife and Habitat," 2010. www.defenders.org.

Richard A. Feeley, Christopher L. Sabine, and Victoria J. Fabry, "Carbon Dioxide and Our Ocean Legacy," National Oceanic and Atmospheric Administration, April 2006. www.pmel .noaa.gov.

Erik Hofmeister et al., "Climate Change and Wildlife Health: Direct and Indirect Effects," US Geological Survey National Wildlife Health Center, March 2010. www.nwhc.usgs.gov.

Katherine Mehl, "Understanding Waterfowl—The Curious Lives of Sea Ducks," *Ducks Unlimited Magazine*, January– February 2004. www.ducks.org.

National Oceanic and Atmospheric Administration, "A Paleo Perspective on Abrupt Climate Change," *NOAA Paleoclimatology*, August 20, 2008. www.ncdc.gov.

National Resources Defense Council, "The Consequences of Global Warming on Wildlife," 2010. www.nrdc.org.

National Wildlife Federation, "The Chesapeake Bay and Global Warming: A Paradise Lost for Hunters, Anglers, and Outdoor Enthusiasts?" September 2007. www.nwf.org.

Robert E. Stewart, Jr., "Technical Aspects of Wetlands: Wetlands as Bird Habitat," *United States Geological Survey Water Supply Paper 2425*, September 7, 2007. www.usgs.gov.

University Corporation for Atmospheric Research, "Climate Model Links Higher Temperatures to Prehistoric Extinction," August 24, 2005. www.ucar.edu.

University of Leeds, "Ozone Healing Could Cause Further Climate Warming," *Science Daily*, January 26, 1010. www.sciencedaily.com.

Thomas Veblen, "New Study Links Western Tree Mortality to Warming Temperatures, Water Stress," University of Colorado at Boulder News Center, January 22, 2009. www.colorado.edu.

Web Sites

Coral Reef Research (www.coralreefresearch.org) Charlie Veron's Web site detailing the present-day destruction of coral reefs because of climate change. Includes video footage and PowerPoint presentations.

National Aeronautics and Space Administration *Earth Observatory* (earthobservatory.nasa.gov) A comprehensive overview of global warming and how it will affect life on the earth.

National Audubon Society (www.audubon.org) Web site of the leading bird conservation organization in the United States; includes many studies on the impact of global warming upon bird populations.

National Wildlife Federation (www.nwf.org) This site offers an extensive section on the effects of global warming upon wildlife populations from one of the best-known wildlife advocacy groups in the United States.

RealClimate: Climate Science from Climate Scientists (www .realclimate.org) An up-to-date site by working climatologists whose goal is to disseminate accurate information about climate change to news media and the public.

Union of Concerned Scientists (www.ucsusa.org) Web site features an extensive section on global warming, including FAQs, maps, illustrations, and clear explanations of the science and impact of global climate change.

United Nations Framework Convention on Climate Change (unfccc.int) A UN site that features the most recent research on climate change from a global perspective. Includes fact sheets, news releases, and an explanation of the United Nations' role in the mitigation of and adaptation to global warming.

United States Global Change Research Program (www.global change.gov) A US governmental agency Web site that integrates climate research with potential solutions for global change. Includes publications, overviews, and fact sheets.

Index

About the Author

Diane Andrews Henningfeld, Ph.D., writes frequently on contemporary issues and literature. A longtime faculty member at Adrian College, she holds the rank of professor emerita. An avid walker, she hiked the 95-mile-long West Highland Way in 2010 and the 76-mile-long Great Glen Way in 2009, both in Scotland. She and her husband divide their time between homes in Adrian, Michigan, and Duck, North Carolina.